D0498376

# RESPECT

*To my wife, Rhonda, whose unflinching support over the past thirty-seven years has made it possible for me to pursue my career dreams.*

Jack Wiley

*To my husband, Aaron, who never questioned my decision to write a book during our first year of parenthood, and to my daughter, Sophie, who is quickly learning what my parents taught me while rocking out to the Rolling Stones—you can't always get what you want, but if you try, sometimes you find you get what you need.*

Brenda Kowske

# RESPECT

Delivering Results by Giving
Employees What They Really Want

Jack Wiley and Brenda Kowske

JOSSEY-BASS
A Wiley Imprint
www.josseybass.com

Published by Jossey-Bass
A Wiley Imprint
989 Market Street, San Francisco, CA 94103-1741—www.josseybass.com

Jossey-Bass books and products are available through most bookstores. To contact Jossey-Bass directly call our Customer Care Department within the U.S. at 800-956-7739, outside the U.S. at 317-572-3986, or fax 317-572-4002.

Wiley also publishes its books in a variety of electronic formats and by print-on-demand. Some material included with standard print versions of this book may not be included in e-books or in print-on-demand. If the version of this book that you purchased references media such as CD or DVD that was not included in your purchase, you may download this material at http://booksupport.wiley.com. For more information about Wiley products, visit www.wiley.com.

**Library of Congress Cataloging-in-Publication Data**

Wiley, Jack
  Respect: delivering results by giving employees what they really want / Jack Wiley and Brenda Kowske.—1st ed.
      p. cm.
    Includes bibliographical references and index.
    ISBN 978-1-118-02781-3 (hardback); ISBN 978-1-118-12401-7 (ebk);
  ISBN 978-1-118-12402-4 (ebk); ISBN 978-1-118-12403-1 (ebk)
    1. Employee motivation. 2. Employee attitude surveys. I. Kowske, Brenda, 1974- II. Title.
      HF5549.5.M63W54 2012
      658.3′14--dc23

                                                                    2011025360

Printed in the United States of America
FIRST EDITION
*HB Printing*    10  9  8  7  6  5  4  3  2  1

# CONTENTS

# LIST OF FIGURES AND TABLES

**I**N 1985, I WAS the director of organization research services for Business Advisors, the consulting firm subsidiary of the former Control Data Corporation. In that role I was responsible for overseeing the delivery of employee survey systems to both Control Data and to our various corporate clients. This was relatively early in my professional career (see the picture that follows from that time period and compare it to the one you find on the inside back flap of this book). While it may seem incredible now, during that era employee survey instruments of 150 to 200 questions were commonplace. What were we thinking?

Even then, during my early data-obsessed days, I must admit the notion of such incredibly long employee surveys seemed a bit ridiculous. Those surveys would often take the average respondent 45 to 60 minutes to complete. Then, when the results were compiled, what do you do with the resulting mountain of data? How do you make sense of it all? That got me to thinking: What is it that we really want to know? If we view the survey as a communication channel with employees, what is it that we really want to learn from them? Instead of asking employees about every possible organizational topic "under the sun," why not just ask them the things we really want to know that we cannot otherwise determine?

But what was it that we really wanted to know? Back then, employee surveys were almost always "employee satisfaction" surveys. I know, thankfully, that our employee survey purposes and tools have progressed a long way since then. But in the 1970s and 1980s surveys were primarily undertaken to help personnel executives and managers, first and foremost, and secondarily, line executives and managers, to better understand what made employees satisfied. But if that was the case, why not just ask them about the elements of organizational life that most drove their levels of satisfaction? Certainly that would not take 150 to 200 questions.

Enter WorkTrends™. About that time, I developed and implemented a survey program that eventually became known as WorkTrends. Its initial purpose was to create a true national normative database of employee opinions on topics most typically asked in employee surveys. We conducted WorkTrends with a sample drawn from a panel of households in the United States, reflective of the nation's population of working adults. Because of the way the panel was constructed and the sample drawn, we had a representative sampling of worker opinions for every major industry group and job type. We also ensured it was representative of all age groups and of both genders.

WorkTrends was created to give us national norms we could use as a benchmark against which we could compare client results. Since we controlled the content of the WorkTrends survey, it could also be used as a research tool. Aha. Why not use WorkTrends to ask employees about what they really wanted? Certainly we could use the answers to that question to help us build a framework for building more efficient employee satisfaction surveys. So that is what I did. Beginning in 1985, I added to WorkTrends this open-ended question:

"As an employee, what is the most important thing you want from the company for which you work?"

Knowing we would need samples from more than one year to draw reliable conclusions about what employees really wanted, I decided to simply grow the database. I knew eventually we would analyze these data and build our framework for a more efficient employee satisfaction survey.

Life happens. Along with my boss at the time, Gail Gantz, we purchased the assets of the survey business from Control Data Corporation and founded Gantz Wiley Research, which opened its doors December 1, 1986. We took WorkTrends with us. With that, my priorities changed. Now I was a company owner with clients to serve, employees to pay, and a business to grow. Although Gail left the company in 1990, the company fortunately continued to grow and expand. Eventually I sold the business to Kenexa, my current employer, in 2006. The now twenty-year-old WorkTrends survey and database came with me.

Over the past two and a half decades, guided by a variety of different influences, employee surveys have changed dramatically. There were several practitioners both inside and external to organizations who helped bring that about. We are glad employee surveys evolved. That became the topic of a book I published last year entitled *Strategic Employee Surveys*.

While all of that was going on, though, I was still collecting answers to my question. In fact, with Kenexa's deeper R&D pockets, we began asking employees in several countries about what they most wanted from their employers. Finally, it was time to do something with that growing mound of data. Along with my co-author, Brenda Kowske, and one of our research associates, Rena Rasch, we analyzed the data. What we learned is revealed in this book.

While I started this effort with an entirely different purpose in mind, I hope you will find the outcome worthwhile. We have learned at least two things: (1) what employees really want and (2) why it matters. Those organizations that pay attention to employee needs are the ones that prosper the most and outperform and outlive their competitors. We invite you to consider our analysis and our conclusions. It boils down to this: all employees are "askin' for is a little r-e-s-p-e-c-t." Find out why it matters so much to them and why it should matter to you.

July 2011                                                                        Jack Wiley
                                                                      La Fontaine, Indiana

# ACKNOWLEDGMENTS

**I AM INDEBTED** to several colleagues and co-workers. I mention first my former business partner, Gail Gantz. Very early in its existence, Gail invested in and helped establish and grow the WorkTrends survey, without which there would be no mountain of data to analyze and no book to write. Many of my former colleagues at Gantz Wiley Research also helped keep alive this special research program, especially Bruce Campbell, Scott Brooks, and Kyle Lundby.

Since I joined Kenexa, several colleagues have provided great operational support and assistance, including Jennifer Meyer, Louise Raisbeck, and Mary Ellen Weber. One co-worker who deserves special attention is Rena Rasch. Rena's research skills proved invaluable in determining the correct research methods for data analysis, and she also generated great research insights, helping us shine a light on what otherwise may have remained hidden. The contributions of two external researchers, Jennifer Elving and Megan Ciampa, also proved quite valuable in the writing of this book.

Several Kenexa executives provided the needed organizational context and support to complete this project. Special recognition is due to Rudy Karsan, Troy Kanter, Don Volk, Sarah Teten, and Eric Lochner. Without their belief in this project and ongoing investment, the database might still be awaiting analysis. I also want to thank Tony Cockerill, who helped us frame our recommendations for future leaders, and John Galvin, who played a very important editing role for this book.

Of course, this book would not exist without the participation of over 175,000 employees from around the world who have completed our surveys.

Finally, I want to thank Brenda Kowske, who proved once again the old adage that two heads are better than one. The opportunity to work with Brenda introduced novel ideas and different ways of discussing our research findings that help animate the main points of this book. For that, and for many other contributions from Brenda, I am very grateful.

# RESPECT

# 1

# What Employees Really Want

**H**ERE'S A SCENARIO that almost any manager, at any level, can relate to. You have a project due and it's requiring a big push from everyone involved. Millions in revenue are at stake. Your career, and your team's success, depend on the project being completed on time and in perfect condition. No problem, you think. You've done this before, but now one of your key team members—a direct report—is threatening to quit. The team member feels undervalued, underappreciated, and underpaid for what's being asked. If you lose this employee at this time, your project is doomed. What next?

Finding a replacement who can do the job on such short notice is out of the question. You need to fix this. You *have* to fix this. The project's success depends on it, and your own career depends on it.

But *how* do you fix it?

This turnover drama is no small matter, and it's one that is played out every day, in every industry, in every country around the world. In nearly every organization—be it small businesses, non-profit organizations, or multinational companies—human capital costs can exceed 40 percent of corporate expenses.[1] Employees represent a massive investment, one that leaders know needs to be protected. It's not simply about avoiding the cost, distraction, and hassle of finding new employees—although those are valid issues. Making sure employees are fulfilled at work isn't just about simple human decency either, although that's also a great argument.

The fact is that managers and organizations that give their employees what they want *outperform* those that don't. As we'll see in Chapter 2, the evidence for providing employees with what they want is incredibly compelling. Figuring out exactly what it is that employees want can be more challenging, but that is exactly what we've spent the last twenty-five years getting to the bottom of. In the process we have amassed a research database unlike any other, and it all started with this simple question:

> "What is the most important thing you want from the organization for which you work?"

Beyond that original and fundamental question we've since added over one hundred additional items that probe topics like leadership effectiveness, employee engagement, diversity practices, turnover and retention, the impact of layoffs, union vulnerability, and job satisfaction. We have answers from all corners of the world, from all job types, from men and women, and from employees who span the working generations. Since we started our research, we've heard from over two hundred thousand employees. In our most recent survey alone, we heard from more than thirty-five thousand employees who work in some of the world's most powerful economies, including Canada, China, Brazil, France, Germany, India, Italy, Japan, Russia, Spain, the United Kingdom, and the United States. The survey's geographic reach actually expands even further, but these countries alone account for an incredible 71 percent of the world's gross domestic product (GDP).[2]

It's not just geographic diversity that we're after. We surveyed employees who work in every major industry, from food to finance, from heavy manufacturing to health care, from retail to pharmaceuticals, and from energy to electronics. We heard from senior U.S. executives in the restaurant business and from construction laborers in Italy. We surveyed retail managers in India and banking managers from the United Kingdom. Our database lets us compare how retail sales associates in, say, Japan match up against those in Canada—or against the rest of the world. How do government workers in Australia feel compared to their counterparts in China? We have that, too.

Not only has this mountain of data been subjected to ongoing and rigorous scientific analysis, but after two and a half decades of compounded knowledge it has allowed us to reveal the basic truths about employee needs and desires.

### R-E-S-P-E-C-T: "Find out what it means to me"

All I'm askin'
Is for a little respect...."

Business books don't generally begin by singing along with the Queen of Soul, Aretha Franklin, but frankly we couldn't have come up with a better entrée—or a more perfectly suited acronym. Your employees are definitely singing this tune, and we don't mean at karaoke night. If you've hired the right people, then you know they have what *you* need. But what do *they* need? The answer can be broken down into seven fundamental desires that include:

*Recognition:* A pat on the back from managers and the organization at-large

*Exciting work:* A job that's interesting, challenging, and fun

*Security of employment:* Job security, you may not want to talk about this, but employees do

*Pay:* Fair compensation for a day's work

*Education and career growth:* Opportunities to develop skills and a career

*Conditions at work:* A workplace that is comfortable physically and socially, and well-equipped

*Truth:* Frank, honest, and transparent leaders

RESPECT means a job that offers employees something they enjoy doing and a chance to shine. Employees are looking for stability and security now (financially and otherwise), and a clear path for their occupational futures. They want the truth—to know what is going on so they can make the best decisions for themselves and their families. Build this organization—one that offers employees the whole package—and employees will work harder, stay longer, and help the organization outperform its competitors.

It's important to realize at the outset that it's not all about the money. Before we started this project, we assumed that the vast majority of employees would primarily want one thing: more pay. The small remainder, we suspected, would be sprinkled across the other categories, but the results, shown in Figure 1.1, indicate that this is definitely not so. It's true that pay comes out on top, with 25 percent of employees saying it is the most important thing to them. Yet, recognition comes in a close second—with 20 percent citing that as their foremost want—and security is right behind, with 18 percent saying it's their most important work need.

This is, frankly, nothing short of incredible news. Think about it. That means 75 percent of what employees want is not directly tied to a fatter paycheck. It means that executives, managers, and organizations have powerful solutions other than salary and benefits to motivate, engage, and retain employees.

## Figure 1.1. Global Results: What Employees Really Want

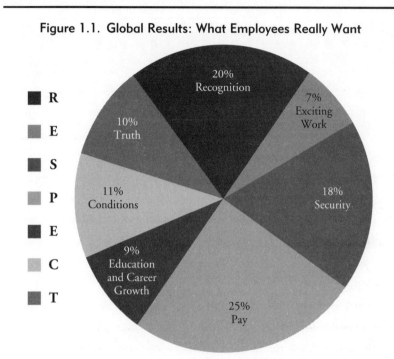

R
E
S
P
E
C
T

20%
Recognition

7%
Exciting
Work

10%
Truth

11%
Conditions

18%
Security

9%
Education
and Career
Growth

25%
Pay

In Chapters 3 through 9 we're going to explore each area of RESPECT individually. We'll show you ways to diagnose your organization's current state of RESPECT, offer you some guiding principles for improving RESPECT, and, finally, give you some concrete actions with proven examples that you can use to increase RESPECT. For now, let's take a quick look at the seven RESPECT principles. For managers who are highly in tune with their workforce, many of these will immediately resonate. What's different today is that we now have the research and the tools to accurately measure, explain, and understand these employee needs and to create a better, more productive workplace.

## Recognition

It is so simple really: just tell employees they've done a good job. When we pore through the responses in this category, employees typically say they want things like: "to be appreciated for the work I do,"

## FINDING SELF-RESPECT: THE CASE OF THE BATTERED TRAINEE

On a recent road trip I stopped in at a fast food restaurant. It was about 2:00 p.m. and there was only one other patron there, and he was reading the newspaper while his French fries got cold and clammy. As I approached the counter, a ponytailed skinny girl of sixteen or so glanced up and offered me a tired, "pity-me" sort of smile.

Her badge announced that her name was Amy, and tacked on underneath, "trainee." Poor Amy; in an effort to elicit compassion from the customer, the organization had branded Amy as slow and dimwitted. I wondered how long she'd have to wait to qualify for her credentials.

Typically, when I see that badge, depending on how hurried I am, I either (a) pretend I forgot something and step back fifteen feet so I can covertly change cashiers or (b) revert back to my coaching days and offer unsolicited feedback: "You're doing a great job!" However, on this particular day, my choice was forced—there were no other cashiers, and I was the only person ordering. C'est la vie.

I purposefully approached the counter and ordered a Number 3. She pressed a button. It beeped. Apparently, this was not the response she had hoped for. She tried again—beep. And again. She muttered an apology and I said, "It's ok." She glared at the cash register for quite some time, although I was sure that the stink-eye and a hard stare wouldn't convince it to do her bidding. As Amy held her finger poised above the button, I held my breath for the sake of her dignity, but no—beep. Defeated, she called Glenda over.

Now, there was no "trainee" apology on Glenda's nametag. With an air of superiority, Glenda emerged from the bowels of the grill area. Glasses blurred with grease, Glenda reminded me of a soldier who has seen a lot of action at the front lines. She was the top dog on this shift.

Glenda clomped over, her gait possibly powered by kinetic energy generated by her fantastic eye rolls. As Glenda instructed Amy on how to right the wrong, it was clear that my trainee had made an error so egregious that the world might just spin right off its axis. Glenda also drove the point home that Amy may be the most stupid employee who ever graced the front counter with her presence. Amy looked so small that she might have crawled into the cash drawer had space allowed. I considered kidnapping her and taking her with me.

At the very least, Amy was most certainly not getting what she needed from her organization. Relationships don't tend to work if one person perceives they are more important than the other. It's a reciprocal engagement, and one that needs to be in balance. Employees give their employer their time, energy, knowledge, and skills. The employer owes them something in return.

Enter RESPECT. Could Amy's hourly wage be motivating enough for her to put up with Glenda's abuse? Unlikely. Plenty of other places pay minimum wage. If Amy likes her job at all, she must have a value in one of the other elements of RESPECT that provide a strong reason to stay despite the verbal floggings doled out by her half-wit supervisor.

Finally, a note to organizations who brand their newcomers as "trainees"—train them as fast as possible! Nothing like starting out at a new job by being embarrassed all day.

—Brenda Kowske

"true recognition, not a good job postal card," and "recognition for the job I've done, and a valid interest in my concerns."

There are a million ways to be busy and overwhelmed at work, so much so that it can be tough to look back and give someone a pat on the back. We are so quick to move to the next challenge that taking a moment to recognize what went right and who was responsible gets lost in the shuffle. Yet, our data clearly indicate that making recognition happen is important to employees. Managers should *make* the time for recognition and thoroughly integrate it into the normal routine.

## Exciting Work

Exciting work means being driven by the result—a result in which both the employee and the organization are heavily committed. Leaders understandably hope that employees make a personal commitment to an organization's financial goals, but employees often get excited by more altruistic goals. I want "a job I can believe in and know that I am making a difference in the world" is a typical response we see. To the employee, exciting work also means being good at the job and, in the words of one employee, the "opportunity to use [the] talents and skills I possess." It includes having a sense of responsibility and autonomy at work so they can satisfy their personal goals for success. An exciting job is filled with assignments that give employees a sense of accomplishment upon completion. Or, as another employee put it, [I want] "the pleasure of working on something that satisfies me."

## Security of Employment

Let's face it: working through 2007 to 2011 was a roller-coaster experience for employees around the world. Those who reported that security was their most important desire said they wanted "stable work without threat of downsizing," to be kept "employed as long as possible," and they don't want to "worry about losing [their] jobs." In the wake of the recent recession, employees are certainly focused on stability and the hope that the dust has begun to settle. Yet, over the past twenty-five years of research, we've seen that the desire for security remains high during both boom and bust economic cycles.

## Pay

No one will be surprised to see this category show up in RESPECT. Being paid for time and effort is one of the most fundamental economic exchanges there is. The pay category actually includes not only salary but also bonuses and benefits—the total compensation package. Although the term "pay for performance" is ubiquitous, in many cases, pay is a "hygiene factor": an employee needs to be paid *enough*, but beyond that point it loses much of its motivating power.[3] However, stopping short of "enough" deeply affects employees' sense of good-will at work, striking a severe blow to employees' commitment to their jobs and organizations. The trick is to identify what employees feel is *fair* pay. As we'll see in Chapter 6, if employees feel good about what they are paid, then an organization has fulfilled this motivating force. It's at this point that managers need to address the other factors that influence employee performance. It's worth repeating: pay is important, but performance is not just about the money.

# Education and Career Growth

Luckily, employees want to learn in their current jobs and also advance in their careers. Promoting this is a no-brainer for leaders. People who noted that education and career growth were important to them said they wanted things like: "continual development of my skills to reach my career goals," "promotional opportunities," "career progression," and "an avenue for advancement."

Providing all that is easier said than done. In an ideal world, employees would learn and grow out of their jobs at the same rate, so that a position is always available—a constant shift upward. We all know that, in actuality, each employee has unique motivations, learning styles, and abilities. Employees become bored or advance at different rates. Many organizations lack a talent-management system that can organize employees' careers and development. In fact, many organizations don't develop career growth programs because they expect employees to take the initiative as part of their advancement. The result can be a confused workplace in which neither employee nor manager knows how to satisfy the need for education and career growth. What might be a worse scenario? Valued employees take initiative and find career growth at a different organization.

## Conditions at Work

We don't work in a vacuum; what happens around us matters. When employees identify positive working conditions as the most important thing they want, they identify two areas of concern. We expected the first category: *physical* working conditions. This deals with the employee's literal surroundings, and here employees highlight issues like "better ventilation and air quality" or "healthy and safe work environment." Physical working conditions have health ramifications ranging from black lung to less-fatal-but-still-painful carpal tunnel syndrome. We were surprised when a larger percentage of employees made comments highlighting "a friendly work environment" and "real work/life balance" and "less stress"; these issues are what we call *social* working conditions.

This should be good news for managers, since creating a positive social environment can be a lot easier to implement than costly changes to the office or factory floor. However, as any manager knows, repairing interpersonal and team dynamics is a sticky wicket, a difficult task due to the emotional nature of the problem. Chapter 8 explores more about how to improve both sets of working conditions.

## Truth

Truth established between two people comes in one, and only one, form: honest communication. When it comes to this type of communication, employees cited two basic types. First, employees want leaders who are direct, open, and honest, as reported in comments asking for "open communication about goals and direction," "truthfulness," and a "clear direction for the company as a whole." Second, their desire for honest feedback and clear goal setting was expressed in comments like "feedback, both positive and corrective" and "a clear definition of responsibilities and expectations."

Organizations ask employees to be completely committed to their work, but without accurate information about where the company is headed, employees are hesitant to give 100 percent or even believe in their organizations. Employee perceptions of dishonesty and lack of transparency (even if the perceptions are not true) breed skepticism and distrust. Rebuilding this trust is mandatory for repairing employee engagement and commitment. This is the case in any economic environment, but it is particularly true following the turbulence caused by the recent recession. Truth is foundational.

# How to Use This Book

Leaders and managers reading this book have probably already realized that their organizations have strength areas that align to RESPECT. Most likely, there are also areas that could be improved. Helping companies respond to their employees' needs is why we've written this book. It's the result of a lifetime of work, research, and commitment on our part. We've pursued it because of our curiosity and because we want to help both employers and employees—and, really, we're all employees.

As you will see in Chapter 2, RESPECT is great for customers and business. To help us make the jump from individual employee wants to a stronger workforce and greater business success, we use Chapters 3 through 9 to examine each tenet of RESPECT in detail, sharing our twenty-five years of research in this field. Each of these chapters starts off with a fictional story about a typical employee dealing with a specific RESPECT issue. These archetypes are composites based on our research. Like our employee base, they live all over the world and have a wide range of jobs—from an executive in the U.S. to an operational employee in a bustling Chinese retail grocery chain. Wherever they live and whatever they do, we think you'll be able to identify with them, their hopes, desires, and aspirations. You probably have people who are grappling with similar issues at your organization. Not only will Chapters 3 through 9 enable you to properly identify each area of RESPECT, but we also provide benchmark data and a wide range of tools to help diagnose potential problem areas that may exist in your organization. Once you've identified your strengths and weaknesses, each chapter also has a set of solutions—with real-world examples that can be used to improve RESPECT.

In Chapter 10 we'll take a peek into the future. It may seem hard to believe, given the state of the global economy over the past few years, but as the economy springs back to life there are strong indicators that we're on the verge of an international talent war. Not only will companies be competing with each other in the consumer marketplace, but they're going to be competing for skilled employees. In this chapter we'll lay out our case for why organizations that want to survive and thrive in the future will need to embed the elements of RESPECT into their workplaces or risk being left behind.

Some of you will end up reading from cover to cover, while others among you will cherry-pick based on your immediate needs and interests. Either way is fine with us. At the end of the book you'll also find a RESPECT diagnostic worksheet that can help you determine your organization's areas of vulnerability. We look forward to hearing about your success and hopefully including your story in our next edition.

# 2

# Why You Should Care

**W**HY SHOULD ORGANIZATIONS provide employees with what they want? Why should organizational leaders care? In some circles giving employees what they want is counterintuitive; that is, everything given to employees is something that is taken away from the organization as a whole. In this worldview, employees and management are on opposite teams, each trying to gain an advantage over the other. You might think of boxers circling one another in the ring, but without weight class. In one corner is the organization, big and brawny but relatively slow due to its heft. In the other corner is the employee, flighty, agile, and lean—especially after economic hard times and a diet of diminished investment in human capital. They circle each other, the employee bouncing around, the organization wishing he or she would just stay put.

This vision is a fallacy, and a harmful one at that. It can be a serious impediment to running an organization effectively. Let us be absolutely

clear at the outset: *there is no "us" versus "them" in this book.* As you'll
see, our employees' demands are fundamentally and almost always very
reasonable. Even more importantly, giving employees what they want is
the same thing that enables organizations to be successful.

## How Does Giving Employees What They Want Help Organizations?

Let's look again at our initial research question: What is the most important thing you want from the organization for which you work? Many
workers responded that they want "a pat on the back." They also want
the "organization to value the work I do" and to provide "recognition."
Providing recognition, formally or informally, gives employees positive
feedback and incrementally directs their behavior. In other words, using
"the carrot" (as opposed to "the stick") motivates employees to take
the very actions management wants. Recognize the right behaviors, and
employees will support business goals.

Even compensation, despite its reputation for being inherently con-
tentious, is not necessarily an "us vs. them" issue. We can start by
questioning the fundamental assumption that makes the topic divisive:
employees always want more money and organizations always want to
pay less. This is not necessarily true. When you talk to employees, they
say they want to be paid what they are *worth.* They want to make enough
money to support their lifestyles, of course, but actual salary negotiations
are about fairness and value. Transparency about the salary decisions—
salary ranges and requirements for raises, for example—helps employees
set realistic expectations and creates an environment of fairness.

We've also seen that employees will accept job offers on the lower end
of the salary range if they include other rewards, and if the job satisfies
the candidate's RESPECT requirements. The new hire is happier and
more motivated to work, while the long-term savings to the company
can be enormous.

Take this example. Let's say a professional services firm with seven
hundred employees is able to hire new recruits for $5,000 less in salary

than their average competitor's salary for the job. They can do this and still attract top talent because the company has created a work environment wherein employee needs are met and they have a stellar reputation (they usually go hand-in-hand). In the United States, you can add in an $850 reduction in payroll taxes, which means a gross annual savings of $5,850 per employee. If we apply that savings to an annual turnover rate of 25 percent, as staff is replaced over the year, the organization has the potential to save $1.02 million in the first year alone; a savings compounded annually by raises applied to lesser salaries. That's quite a bit of cash that can be reinvested in employee programs or allocated to other strategic initiatives.

In the rest of this chapter, we will demonstrate how providing employees with RESPECT—with the things they really want—yields tangible benefits to organizations. The next section has plenty of indices, data, and graphs, but the upshot is this: *RESPECT is strongly, positively and significantly related to organizational success, whether that is defined by the employee, customer, or financial stakeholder.* It also leads to more fulfilling, rewarding lives—and the value of that is priceless.

## RESPECT Engages Employees

Employees who get what they want from their organizations are more engaged than their unfulfilled counterparts. What is employee engagement and why is it important to your organization's success? Intuitively we all know what it means to be engaged in our work, but for the purposes of this book we will use a precise definition. Employee engagement is:

> "The extent to which employees are motivated to contribute to organizational success, and are willing to apply discretionary effort to accomplishing tasks important to the achievement of organizational goals."[1]

Enthusiasm for work, commitment, organizational pride, alignment with organizational goals, and a willingness to exert discretionary effort are all elements that show up in past research on employee engagement.[2,3,4,5] The level of employee engagement is important because it is strongly related to a host of outcomes such as individual and team performance, customer satisfaction, profitability, and total shareholder return. Simply put, organizations with a more engaged workforce consistently outperform their competitors.

Does having more RESPECT in an organization relate to more engaged employees? Our data say "yes." Using the Kenexa Employee Engagement Index (EEI) we quantify engagement by measuring pride, satisfaction, advocacy, and commitment. The rationale is straightforward: employees who have pride in and are satisfied in their organization also tend to advocate for and remain with their organization.[6] Specifically, the EEI includes these four items:

- "I am proud to tell people I work for my organization."
- "Overall, I am extremely satisfied with my organization as a place to work."
- "I would recommend this place to others as a good place to work."
- "I rarely think about looking for a new job with another organization."

Employees answer these questions using a standard five-point balanced Likert agreement scale (that is, for each question respondents mark strongly agree, agree, neither agree nor disagree, disagree, or strongly disagree). The EEI score is the average percent of agreement across the four components of the index; the EEI score is thus presented in terms of "percent favorable."[7]

For the analysis presented in Figure 2.1, we first segmented employees by their most important want (pay, security, etc.). Using our WorkTrends survey, we then sorted employees into two simple categories: those who get what they want and those who do not. For each group we computed an EEI score. Not surprisingly, we found that employees whose RESPECT needs are fulfilled also have a very high EEI score: 76 percent. They outscore their unfulfilled counterparts by an incredible thirty-one percentage points. High levels of employee engagement should be a goal for all organizations, and one way to guarantee it is to provide RESPECT.

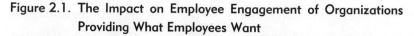

Figure 2.1. The Impact on Employee Engagement of Organizations Providing What Employees Want

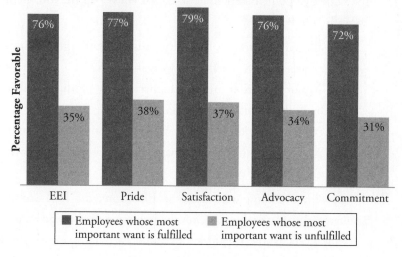

## RESPECT Supports Superior Performance

In addition to impacting employee engagement, employees who get what they want from their organizations also view their organizations as more formidable competitors. As you can imagine, the organization holds a tremendous advantage when its employees truly believe they are on a "winning team."

Employees are the eyes and ears of an organization, and their perceptions provide valuable insight into how well things are working. Do you want to know what your suppliers and customers think of your business? Just ask your employees. Previous research has demonstrated that employees' ratings of organizational practices and procedures correlate positively and significantly with the perceptions of external stakeholders, particularly those of customers.[8] As a result, employee perceptions of customer service quality can serve as a "proxy" for actual ratings of customer satisfaction and loyalty.

We put this to the test by measuring employees' perceptions of their organizations' overall customer service, quality, competitiveness, and performance, using the Performance Outcome Index (POI).[9] In our WorkTrends survey, we ask employees to rate their organizations (using the same five-point Likert scale described above) on the four items that comprise the POI:

- "Overall, customers are very satisfied with the products and services they receive from my organization."
- "My organization provides higher quality products and services than other similar organizations."
- "My organization competes well against others in the industry."
- "My organization's performance has improved during the past year."

As with the computation of the EEI score, the POI score is the average percent favorable score on the items comprising the index.

Employees whose organizations fulfill their most important wants also report that their organization is well positioned for success (see Figure 2.2). The POI score for fulfilled employees is 74 percent, a

---

**Figure 2.2. The Impact on Operational Performance of Organizations Providing What Employees Want**

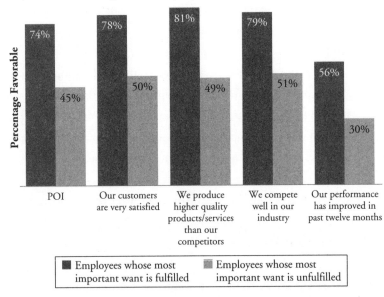

remarkable twenty-nine percentage points higher than the unfulfilled group. This difference between the two groups is notably similar across each of the four components of the POI. Employees are not only telling us that organizations that meet employee needs are more engaging places to work, but that that they are also better at providing higher quality products and services and creating more satisfied customers. These organizations are also viewed as more competitive, and their overall business performance is more likely to have improved in the past year.

## RESPECT Means Satisfied Customers

Of course, you don't have to rely solely on employee opinions of how customers feel about a company. You can find out directly from the customers. We wanted to determine the relationship between organizations fulfilling the RESPECT needs of their employees and the satisfaction of customers who purchase products and services from that organization. We wanted to answer this specific question:

> "Do organizations that do a better job of providing what employees want also create more satisfied customers?"

To answer this question we needed valid and reliable measures of both organizational RESPECT and customer satisfaction. We created a RESPECT Index[10] by identifying rating scale questions contained within our WorkTrends survey that measure the fulfillment of the seven RESPECT categories (see Table 2.1).

To measure customer satisfaction, we relied on an already existing and highly regarded measure, the American Customer Satisfaction Index (ACSI)—an economic indicator based on customer evaluations of U.S. and foreign-owned entities selling products in the United States. Companies use ACSI evaluations to improve and maximize their customer relationships, and this, in turn, drives customer loyalty and profitability. In fact, over the sixteen-year period of the survey, it has been shown that companies with high ACSI scores tend to have better performing stock prices than low ACSI scorers have. The national ACSI average is 75.3

points. Scores above that are viewed as good, and, in general, scores of 80 and above are viewed as excellent. Scores of 70 and below are generally considered an indication that companies need to work on improving their customer relationships.[11]

---

**Table 2.1. The RESPECT Index Items**

| | |
|---|---|
| **Recognition** | My company recognizes productive people. |
| **Exciting Work** | I get excited about my work. |
| **Security** | How do you rate your organization in providing job security for people like yourself? |
| **Pay** | I am paid fairly for the work I do. |
| **Education** | My organization provides me with the opportunity for growth and development. |
| | I can achieve my career goals at this organization. |
| **Conditions** | I feel that I am part of a team. |
| | The stress level at work is reasonable. |
| **Truth** | When my organization's senior management says something, you can believe it's true. |
| | In my organization, there is open, honest two-way communication. |

---

Upon examining more than sixty companies for which we have both RESPECT Index and ACSI scores, we found a very strong positive link between the two indexes (see Figure 2.3). For example, companies that score in the top 20 percent on the RESPECT Index achieve an average ACSI score of 79—almost four points above the national average. This impressive result can be contrasted with the performance of the bottom RESPECT companies. They manage a score of only 67.3.

What does this mean? It means that those organizations that do a better job of fulfilling the most important workplace needs of their employees are the same ones that tend to do a better job (we could say a *much* better job) of fulfilling the needs of their customers. While customer satisfaction alone does not ensure customer loyalty, we know that customer loyalty will not result without customer satisfaction. Loyal customers are not only repeat customers, but they tend to buy more products and services, thus further increasing an organization's revenue and market share.

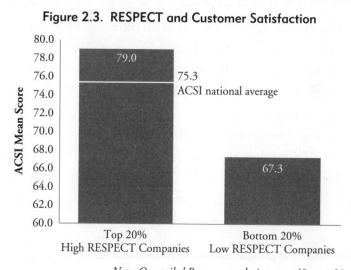

**Figure 2.3. RESPECT and Customer Satisfaction**

*Note: One-tailed Pearson correlation: r = .40, p < .01*

# RESPECT Shows Us the Money

To demonstrate the impact of a high RESPECT workplace, we have so far relied on the opinions of the workers themselves and the organization's customers. That's great, you might be thinking, but what about bottom-line financial performance? Earlier in this chapter we highlighted how high RESPECT companies can save salary expenses over time, but we also wanted to see how these companies performed against their corporate peers. In other words, does it pay to be a high RESPECT organization? Do high RESPECT organizations deliver greater bottom-line business success? Do financial stakeholders stand to benefit more by investing in high RESPECT organizations?

To answer these questions we correlated RESPECT Index scores against three financial metrics: diluted earnings per share (DEPS), total shareholder return (TSR), and return on assets (ROA) for over one hundred companies worldwide. They represent all major industries, including retail, finance and banking, manufacturing, hospitality, health care, and business services, in all major economies around the world. More than 80 percent of the companies studied are multinational, with locations and employees in more than one hundred countries. These companies represent about 10 percent of the Fortune 100. When we looked at these data, the top quintile RESPECT Index companies outperformed both the average and the bottom quintile RESPECT companies on all three of these key measures of financial performance (see Figure 2.4).

Top quintile RESPECT companies, on average produce US $3.56 more DEPS than the bottom quintile of RESPECT companies. For TSR, the results are equally dramatic. During 2009, a time of market volatility and higher than average returns due in part to the bottoming out of the stock market in 2008, high RESPECT companies delivered to their shareholders an average return of 49.8 percentage points more than low RESPECT companies. An examination ROA produces the same conclusion: high RESPECT companies outperform low RESPECT companies by a gaping margin.

We have taken our analysis one step further by quantifying the impact on financial performance of an organization that improves its RESPECT Index score. Think about it this way. If an organization's RESPECT Index score is computed as an average score falling on a scale of "1" (low RESPECT) to "5" (high RESPECT), every .25 RESPECT Index score improvement would correspond, on average, to an additional US $0.58 of DEPS, an additional 7.4 percentage points in TSR, and an increase of .4 percentage points in ROA. Now that is leverage.

We realize these three measures of business performance are complex and primarily used by financial analysts when making decisions on whether to buy, sell, or hold a stock. Because of that, we wanted to

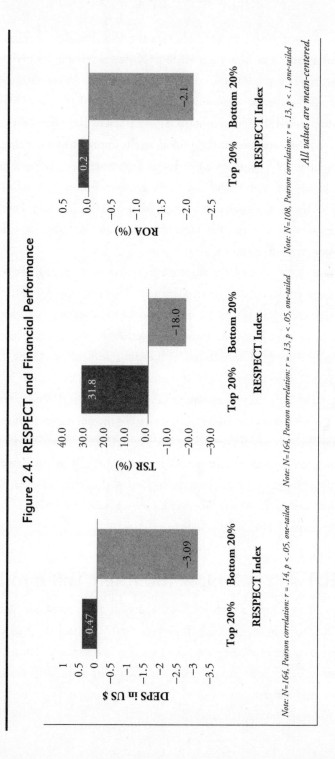

Figure 2.4. RESPECT and Financial Performance

*Note: N=164, Pearson correlation: r = .14, p < .05, one-tailed*

*Note: N=164, Pearson correlation: r = .13, p < .05, one-tailed*

*Note: N=108, Pearson correlation: r = .13, p < .1, one-tailed*

*All values are mean-centered.*

add to our analysis a very tangible measure of financial performance. We therefore looked at how high RESPECT Index companies matched up against blue-chip companies in the stock market. In our first analysis, we compared their six-year stock price increase to that of the Dow Jones Composite Index. The Composite Index tracks sixty-five of the most prominent names in industry, including the entire Dow Jones Industrial Average portfolio, plus the Dow Jones Transportation Average, and the Dow Jones Utility Average. Over a six-year performance period—which includes the recent recession—these high RESPECT Index companies performed on par with the Composite Index and actually outperformed it by one percentage point.

Next, we subjected the stock performance of these high RESPECT Index companies to a more stringent test. After the Dow Jones Industrial Average, the S&P 500 is the most widely followed index of large-cap American stocks. It is considered a bellwether for the American economy and is included in the Index of Leading Indicators. Many mutual funds, exchange-traded funds, and other funds such as pension funds are designed to track the performance of the S&P 500 index. When compared with the S&P 500, the RESPECT Index companies outperformed it, on average, by two percentage points (see Figure 2.5). A 2 percent advantage in stock performance is no small matter, especially when considering that the competition represents the highest-performing, most formidable corporations in the world. There is no way around it: RESPECT at work delivers superior financial results.

# RESPECT—It Is Simply the Right Thing to Do

What does creating a high RESPECT organization give you? We know that it creates more engaged employees, and we know these employees believe they are producing superior products and services. These positive employee beliefs are a proven proxy for actual corporate performance, and we see that reflected in satisfied and loyal customers, superior financial performance, and higher stock prices.

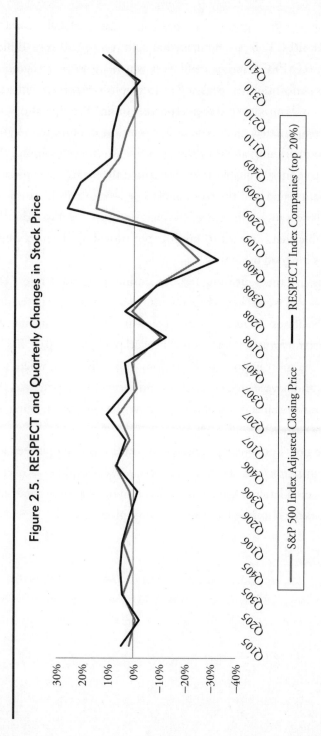

Figure 2.5. RESPECT and Quarterly Changes in Stock Price

S&P 500 Index Adjusted Closing Price
RESPECT Index Companies (top 20%)

One of the great mysteries of today's global workforce is that RESPECT is so fundamental and yet often very difficult to deliver. RESPECT means employees who want to be recognized, who want to perform at their peak and to accomplish their work with a sense of security and confidence in their economic future. Yes, they also want to be fairly compensated. In addition, they want the opportunity to grow and develop their skills, and they want positive working conditions. When it comes to honesty, people at work are no different from people at home: they want to be told the truth and to be able to tell the truth without fear. These wants—these needs—these desires—seem so rational and so reasonable that it's hard to imagine not providing them to employees. And it's for good business!

It is also the right thing to do. Consider the golden rule: "Do unto others as you would have them do unto you." This adage of reciprocity is found in almost all religions and represents the most elemental teaching of respectful human interaction. The workplace, for its part, has become one of the most important institutions in our lives. It's where we make friends and have shared experiences and carry out our potential. As such, don't our workplaces also deserve to have the golden rule hung over the entryway as well?

We now know how important RESPECT is to employees, and also to organizations. In the next chapters we will explore each employee want—each letter of the RESPECT acronym—in more detail and offer solutions for boosting RESPECT at your place of work.

# 3

# Recognition

**M**EET ANN. She is exhausted.

After pulling a swing shift yesterday, this beleaguered twenty-eight-year-old is getting ready to head back to work again this morning. The assisted living facility where she works is called The Meadows, ironic given the concrete jungle in which it is located. It's 7:00 a.m. and Ann hasn't even had time yet for her coffee. There's bad coffee at The Meadows cafeteria, barely the color of weak tea, which doesn't come close to clearing the fog. A stiff cup of coffee isn't the only thing Ann's going to miss today. After a brief pause to lament the loss of her morning shower, she whips her disheveled blond hair back into a ponytail and pulls on her scrubs. Sometimes she wishes there was some variety in her pale blue health-care uniform, but today at least she's thankful they feel just like pajamas. With that she's headed off to work.

"Hi George," says Ann to the elderly man she passes in the hallway. "How are you doing today?" Slightly stooped over his walker, he turns to face her and gives her a blank look. "Were you heading to breakfast? I'm going that way myself," she says. Thankful for the company and perhaps a sense of purpose, George accompanies Ann down the mauve-and-taupe hallway, brushing the silk ferns as he shuffles by.

Ann's schedule can be grueling, but the stress of her job can be so much more than that. Multiply George by one hundred. There are so *many* needs at The Meadows, and as a nursing aide she can only do so much. Usually Ann feels as though she's largely ineffective. While office workers shuffle paper, she shuffles people, trying to meet the seemingly endless needs of residents. Any one attempt to make life better for someone is met with ten other people tugging at her attention. She's forced to move fast, which she feels translates into impersonal and cold conversations with the residents. It's depressing really. The pace of the work means she's running from room to room at breakneck speed, and she's not even aware that the help she's providing is appreciated.

The demands never end, and there's always more to do. After shepherding George to the cafeteria, Ann walks by the head nurse's office. "Can I talk to you in my office?" the nurse asks, lips pursed. A resident's daughter has complained that Ann has a bad attitude, and she also thinks someone has been stealing from her mother. Ann sighs. It's a common complaint at assisted living facilities, and there's nothing she can do.

She is mentally wiped out from hearing only complaints and never any recognition. She is paid next to nothing for a job whose demands never let up. As she's running through her usual defense tactics with her supervisor, anger wells. She thinks about quitting. Enough is enough. There are plenty of assisted living facilities in her town. She can make this kind of money almost anywhere, and maybe she can at least find a place where employees are appreciated.

## The Importance of Feedback and Recognition

The hectic pace of almost any workplace can stretch leaders thin, leaving their direct reports to fend for themselves. As in Ann's story, she and her boss are so busy fighting fires that there's little if any time to review what works and what doesn't and to recognize Ann's talents and expertise.

Our own and others' research agree unequivocally: employees want and need recognition for their hard work. Being appreciated by an organization and its leaders is crucial to employees to feeling good about the work they do, but it is also essential to forming loyalty to an organization[1] and being productive in the long run.[2] It isn't just employees at the lower rungs of the corporate ladder either. All employees—chief marketing officers or maintenance engineers—want to be recognized.

Other research has shown us that balanced feedback—meaning feedback that is both positive and critical—is more likely to motivate employees to improve. Studies have indicated that, in the service sector, recognition improved performance by 15 percent, and when recognition was combined with balanced feedback, performance increased by 41 percent in manufacturing and 30 percent in service sector settings.[3]

Employees from around the world tell us that recognition is sometimes reserved only for the most productive employees, and this turns out to be a fundamental mistake at many organizations. Yes, productive workers deserve recognition, as it's a key motivational tool, but less productive employees also need balanced feedback as a stimulus to work harder, to learn needed skills, and to be more focused on the job. The business logic is clear: by improving recognition to second- and third-tier producers, businesses are more likely to see those employees excel in their jobs and rise to that top tier.

The numbers tell the story of the under-recognized. Less than half (49 percent) of employees worldwide are satisfied with the recognition they receive. More importantly, more than a quarter (26 percent) are *dissatisfied* with the recognition they receive at work. Here is the critical and yet simple point: if providing balanced feedback is essential to motivate employees—and the research is incontrovertible on this—that means that managers are sub-optimizing the performance improvements of at least a quarter of the world's workforce. Therein resides an enormous opportunity for company-wide gains in productivity.

When employees say that recognition is the most important thing they want from their organizations, they mention things like:

- "Recognition and respect"
- "A pat on the back, or some praise would be nice"

- "Recognition when we do a good job—right now it is all about getting chewed out when we mess up"
- "Recognition for the work that I do and more respect from senior management for working diligently and making sacrifices without complaint during this difficult financial time"
- "I want to be respected and recognized as a valuable team member"
- "To be appreciated for the work I do and not be treated like a number and the dollar amounts I make for them"
- "Recognize the contributions of all employees, not just a few; it would help to develop the team spirit and cooperation that are vital for us to succeed in the current economic climate"
- "Acknowledgement for dedication and good work"

Recognition and appreciation, respect and consideration are fundamental desires that we all seek every day, in virtually every facet of our lives. It is not surprising then that recognition and respect are essential on the job as well.

## Is Ann Receiving the Recognition She Deserves?

Ann represents a type of employee—women under thirty who work in health care services—who is more likely to indicate that recognition is needed for her personal success.[4] Nearly half of employees (44 percent) like Ann do not believe they receive sufficient praise or recognition from their bosses. Not only does this represent a huge potential productivity loss, but these same employees are the ones most likely to be less committed to their organizations; these are the employees most likely to quit.

The bottom line is that Ann is a great employee, but if she doesn't start getting the respect and recognition she believes in her heart she deserves, she's going to respond by reducing her efforts on the job—because why bother if efforts aren't appreciated? Or she'll quit. Either choice is a bad one for The Meadows. They will either have to spend time and money hiring and training a new employee or deal with an unmotivated and less productive Ann. Where employees feel that their organization motivates people to work hard and to put in extra effort when needed, 69 percent of employees are also satisfied with their recognition. Where these conditions do not prevail, only 16 percent of employees are satisfied with the recognition they receive.

Just because you may not be in the health care services industry, don't think your organization has escaped the recognition problem. One thing we've learned is that, although electronic manufacturing leads the pack, under-recognition is pervasive in all industries across the globe (see Figure 3.1).

**Figure 3.1. Employee Satisfaction with Recognition by Global Industry**

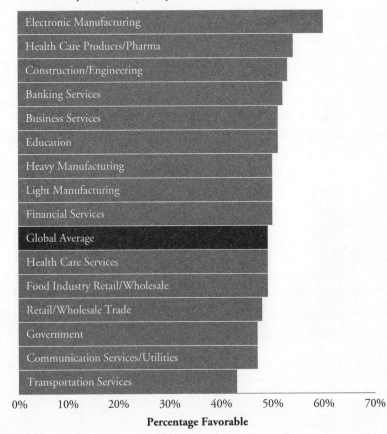

# Recognition: A Key to Great Management

Often, the best form of recognition comes from one's boss. There's nothing like having your manager stop by your office or workspace and say, "Hey, I saw your latest *[insert project/report/work product/etc. here]*. Nice work. That's exactly what we wanted. Thanks." After all, employees spend a good deal of effort trying to please the boss. It's just nice to know that they've succeeded. A mix of hope and pride results; not only is it possible to meet the boss's expectations, but they actually can do it!

Simply put, the role of the manager is absolutely critical in doling out praise. In fact, how employees view their manager's performance is influenced by how managers use recognition. Those who are satisfied with the recognition they receive perceive their managers in a much more favorable light than the under-recognized (see Figure 3.2). This discrepancy shows up in employees' ratings of their managers' overall performance; their people and task management and leadership skills; and their likelihood to keep commitments. Overall, 81 percent of employees who are satisfied with the recognition they receive for the work they do rate their managers as effective, while only 30 percent of

**Figure 3.2. The Impact of Employee Recognition on Views of Managerial Performance**

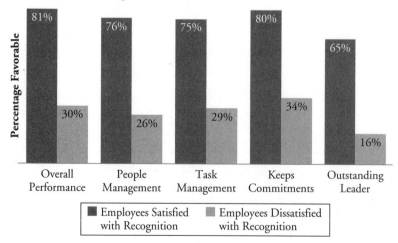

the under-recognized see their managers as effective. The ability to give recognition is the litmus test of good management; such a pervasive element in the role of a manager bleeds into all elements of managerial performance.

# How to Stop Worrying and Love the Millennials

Currently, one of management's biggest looming fears is the impact of Baby Boomer retirement on productivity. Although Generation X has been working for years, the bulk of the Boomers will be replaced by the youthful Millennials. The Millennials, or Gen Y, of course, are the children of Baby Boomers—born between 1980 and 1995—and in the United States there are more than eighty million of them either in the workforce or on the verge of entering it.

Fear drives our fascination with the Millennials; they lack street-savvy, they are naïve, and their college educations have left them unprepared for life as an organizational citizen. If nothing else, they need *training*—training in job skills to be sure, but perhaps more importantly, they need to be trained to be good employees. Basically, akin to the "just got my driver's license, where are the keys to the convertible, Dad" kind of moment, the Boomers are preparing to hand over the keys to their livelihoods to their children. And if you're in the business world, you'd better watch out—at least that's the message from much of the media and high-end business consultants.

As "60 Minutes" correspondent Morley Safer put it for his 2008 segment on the Millennials: "They were raised by doting parents who told them they are special, played in little leagues with no winners or losers, or all winners. They are laden with trophies just for participating and they think your business-as-usual ethic is for the birds. And if you persist in this belief you can take your job and shove it." *Yikes*!

In a 2006 interview on PBS,[5] Stan Smith of Deloitte and Touche USA liberally stereotyped generations at work when he said, "I put it this way. The Baby Boomers are 'work, work, work.' It's a very important part of their lives. Gen X is 'work, work, I want to work some more, let's talk about it.' And Gen Y is 'work, work, you want me to work even more? How lame. I think I'll I.M. my friends and tell them how lame you are, asking me to work even more.'"

Smith went on to say that Generation Y will change the way organizations run, that they will need to have flexible schedules, and that management will only be able to ask them to do personally fulfilling jobs. While the workplace of today will undeniably evolve to accommodate changing technology and demands, as it always does, that isn't necessarily a bad thing. In fact, our research indicates that the Millennials may turn out to be even better employees and, eventually, employers than their predecessors.

Specifically, and despite the hype about needing trophies just for participating, Millennials are more positive about recognition than their elder co-workers. Sixty-four percent of them believe their employers recognize productive people, compared to just 52 percent for Baby Boomers. The majority of them are satisfied with the recognition they personally receive (as opposed to just 46 percent for Boomers). Finally, they are also more likely to believe their organizations value their contributions (see Figure 3.3). That may seem like fluff compared to

**Figure 3.3. Employee Perceptions of Recognition by Generational Group**

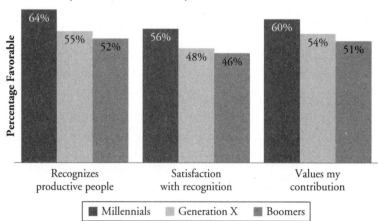

someone used to working in a salt mine, but these are all key indicators for satisfied employees—employees who receive *RESPECT*. Let the data guide you: if organizations continue to create workplaces that enhance recognition, then productivity will follow. You can stop worrying about babying the Millennials.

## Providing Recognition the Right Way

"Compensation is a right; recognition is a gift." That's how the noted author and management consultant, Rosabeth Moss Kanter, once put it when talking about employee relations.[6] Ms. Kanter may have been focusing on the gift of recognition from the perspective of the employee—wow, it feels great to be recognized for my hard work—but the fact is that it's also a gift to the *company*. Not only is providing effective recognition a low-cost technique to engage employees in their work, but it also translates directly into stronger performance and increased profit. It will also increase the likelihood of a valued employee staying on the job—something your CFO will love. Recognition is cheaper and (for most workers, anyway) a more effective technique than exclusively throwing money at the problem. This is an area where the data are absolutely clear: recognizing employees is essential for boosting performance and it is a key driver of retention—especially the retention of high performers.

When recognition comes from the highest levels of an organization, it often has the most significant impact, but it's important that managers at *all* levels learn to properly recognize employees. It's also important to keep in mind that there is no one-size-fits-all solution, and an organization's culture will certainly influence how recognition is delivered. Some employees—and some organizations—may prefer a public show of appreciation, while others may be more satisfied with a private but personal "thank you" or a "job well done." One of our favorite examples of private recognition comes from Michael Lynton, a co-chair of Sony Pictures. He directly calls and writes notes to employees to recognize their good work.[7] This type of behavior from the "top of the house" sends a strong message and is a great model down through the management ranks.

A number of contributing factors impact how employees feel about the recognition they receive. To use an extreme example, recognizing someone's accomplishments as he or she is on the way out the door to another job obviously isn't an effective technique. While it will take some work, supervisors, managers, and executives who understand these issues will be the most effective at recognition and, more broadly, giving job performance feedback. Among the most important are

- *Timeliness*. The shorter the interval between an individual's action and the corresponding recognition, the more powerful the impact will be, so don't wait too long.[8] At the Great American Insurance Group, their High Five program enables employees to earn points on a daily basis and then convert them into gift cards and other prizes. This technique provides instant feedback from managers and also recognition from peers.[9]

- *Specificity*. Recognition that focuses on a specific behavior or performance will be viewed as the most useful by employees.

- *Frequency*. Recognize often and regularly. If your company's recognition only comes during an annual review, that's not enough, and it will have less impact on employees.[10]

- *Fairness and accurateness*. Employees can sense when recognition is simply lip service. When recognition pertains to performance that is verifiable and comes from a respected source, it is more meaningful.[11]

- *Helpfulness*. To be maximally useful, recognition must not only identify the positive outcome, but also help the individual understand how his or her positive action led to it. In short, explain why an action was beneficial.

# How to Diagnose Your Organization's State of Recognition

When employees say, "We only hear the bad news" or "My manager doesn't know what I'm doing or how well I do it" or "I don't see anyone getting recognized for a job well done," the organization has a recognition problem. Before an organization can solve its recognition deficiencies, it must have a good understanding of what is getting in the way of employees feeling recognized, and nothing will help a manager more than a direct, focused discussion with the team. At the outset, managers should seek answers to the following questions:

- Under what circumstances do employees receive feedback at work? How often do they receive feedback?
- Think about a time when employees received feedback that they thought was useful. What made this feedback useful to them?
- What types of recognition have employees received (or seen others receive) at work?
- How frequently is recognition provided?
- What types of recognition do my employees want? Private? Public? A combination of both?

# Guiding Principles and Concrete Actions for Improving Recognition

Once organizations identify their existing state of recognition—its strengths and its weaknesses—then managers and executives can begin executing a recognition strategy and improving their delivery. Those who do so stand to reap significant rewards. Take the example of Symantec Corporation, a California-based software firm that uses a centralized system called the Applause Program, which allows employees to be honored with gift cards totaling up to $1,000 and e-cards to show appreciation. Since program implementation, approximately 65 percent of employees have been touched, and Senior Compensation Analyst Bill McCullough notes that it has greatly impacted employee engagement scores. Beforehand, it was estimated that only 5 percent of employees were recognized for outstanding performance. Now, thanks to the new program, the return on investment in employee recognition can be tracked and job-performance metrics *guarantee* that workers receive the appropriate recognition.[12]

Methods to improve recognizing employees include:

- *Identify employee preferences*. Get to know your employees and you'll learn what they like and what they don't. It seems straightforward, but in many organizations managers know little about their employees and what drives them. Once managers learn what their direct reports value, they can personally tailor recognition practices to needs and interests.

  Putting this concept into practice, the local government of Snohomish County, Washington, created a highly popular and decentralized recognition program, which has grown significantly. In order to show appreciation for their peers, employees draw small, personalized pictures on cards. The county's human resources director believes that "having a little, unique, and artistic way to support others has caused high employee satisfaction." It also inspires mutual learning between the giver and receiver and encourages co-workers to get to know one another.[13]

- *Make informal recognition a habit*. When asked about what kind of recognition or rewards they value, employees often reply that they would simply like to be told "thank you" or "good job," or be given the well-known "pat on the back" for a job well done. Those in supervisory, managerial, and executive positions should make a commitment to use these informal techniques when they see exemplary performance.

  To reinforce the relative value of informal recognition, a study called Rewards at Work investigated how U.S. workers felt toward five reward categories: pay, benefits, the work itself, long-term opportunities for development, and feelings of belonging. The research showed that all five types of rewards were considered *equally* important. Informal recognition techniques, which require little financial investment, also foster a stronger sense of belonging among employees.[14]

- **Communicate success.** Face-to-face communication is ideal, but it's not always possible. That shouldn't stop managers from recognizing their co-workers. Emails, text messages, and even voice mails are all techniques for offering congratulations in a timely way. Technology shouldn't be the only tool, but when face-to-face contact is not possible, it's a great asset.

  Consider the example of Francis Goss, the head of commercial operations at Grass Roots, a marketing, research, and human resource services company in the United Kingdom, who found creative ways to recognize and reward employees through simple means. Giving recognition—and instilling motivation and drive—may seem difficult for a manager who oversees several employees scattered across satellite offices. Goss gets around that problem by listing the names of recognized employees and their contributions on the front page of the firm's internal website. To motivate, he holds weekly conference calls to communicate objectives and incentives for his team. Because it's so direct, instantaneous, and personal, Goss also uses text messaging as a feedback and recognition tool.[15]

- **Establish criteria and clear policies for "formal" recognition programs.** When it comes to recognition, everyone should be playing by the same rules. Employees will be acutely aware, and rightly so, if they aren't evaluated against the same standards or criteria as their colleagues. Formal recognition programs, especially those that include incentive compensation plans, stock awards, and other such financial rewards, should be stated clearly and concisely as policy. Large organizations with operations around the world typically benefit the most from centralized reward programs. Not only will a centralized system allow organizations to reach more employees efficiently, but it also will allow human resource professionals to measure a program's effectiveness and value more easily. Smaller organizations can, of course, act more nimbly and leverage the power and flexibility of a decentralized approach.

Derek Irvine, chief marketing officer and head of strategic consulting at Globoforce, a provider of employee recognition services with headquarters in Dublin, Ireland, and Southborough, Massachusetts, states that a global approach reduces duplication efforts and simplifies the administration.[16]

- *Create opportunities for contact with higher managers.* Its human nature to want to be appreciated by the boss, and it is also a powerful form of strategic recognition. One incredibly effective technique to promote this kind of interaction between senior managers and front-line employees is called "two-downs." The practice simply refers to executives and managers engaging in discussions with employees two levels down in the organization. Cynthia McGague, director of human resources at Coca-Cola, which employs more than ninety thousand people worldwide, has relied on these types of recognition programs even during challenging economic times. Just prior to the 2008 Beijing Olympics, employees were nominated for living the values of the company. Then, two to four representatives from each of the company's geographies worked at the Olympics and had the opportunity to meet and spend time with the CEO. For the 2010 World Cup, they undertook a similar program, but this time nominating employees based on productivity. McGague is a booster of these types of programs, but acknowledges that companies must be selective about how many they do and focus on events or activities that have the highest potential return on investment.[17]

- *Train your managers in recognition practices and techniques.* Like any business skill, training and learning is an essential component to implementing a successful program.

  Consider the example of Everett Clinic, a health care provider in Washington State. Managers there have embraced the concept of doling out small but consistent nods of recognition, which they believe are more effective than formal and glitzy programs and events. Peers and supervisors hand out "Herograms." In 2009 alone, more than 43,000 Herograms were awarded for exceptional accomplishments. Herograms allow employees to win prizes like gift cards or paid days off. Not only do supervisors and employees recognize one another, but the CEO also keeps a stash of gift certificates and coffee cards in his office for immediate recognition. It works. Everett Clinic boasts an overall employee satisfaction rate of over 80 percent and a turnover rate below 13 percent. This sets the company apart from other health care organizations in the Clinic's market area, where the turnover rate is five to ten percentage points higher.[18]

- *When appropriate, use training opportunities as a form of recognition.* The opportunity to improve job-related skills and develop one's career not only makes an employee better at the job, but also greatly enhances engagement with the company. It is also a very potent form of recognition.

  Capital One recently developed a training and recognition program for its "High Value Servicing" call center employees. Agents in this call center receive specialized training, while recognition awards are given quarterly to the top 10 percent of performers. But it doesn't stop there. Employees who aren't necessarily the highest producers, but who have demonstrated outstanding improvement in their own performance, are also honored.[19]

While these techniques have been proven to work, it's also true that what works for one company won't necessarily work as well for another.

This is why tracking the impact of your company's recognition practices is critical. *A failure to do so can backfire.* For example, some unions see recognition programs as a potential source of favoritism and believe they incite jealousy, so finding the right blend between private and public recognition is critical. An Ontario, Canada, Auto Workers Credit Union hosts luncheons or dinners to reward groups of employees who took part in dedicated sales campaigns, according to Janet Letros, the director of human resources. Employees who have gone above and beyond are often recognized behind closed doors, perhaps with a personal visit from the CEO or a letter of acknowledgement.

What are the attributes of the best recognition programs? Over the course of several years we have surveyed the best practices from companies large and small, across almost every single industry, and with anywhere from ten to ten thousand employees. The truth is, of course, that every company is different, with its own unique character, personality, and culture, and yet the key to success often revolves around being creative with recognition programs. Programs that employ elements such as time off or entertaining group activities, even food and gift cards—or something specifically catered to the organization—will almost always provide a high return on investment. These programs will drive higher employee engagement, boost productivity, and add to the bottom line. Several companies are in the business of providing out-of-the-box solutions, and many of these are excellent, but by following the guidelines and actions outlined above, any organization can enhance its recognition practices.

## NO NEWS IS GOOD NEWS: THE TALE OF THE UNDER-THE-RADAR ENGINEER

Years ago when my husband was taking the first steps in his career, he started his first job as an engineer. He was a couple months into his work and was diligently following instructions and being productive. A worker bee to the core, he buzzed from task to task, bringing his new duties to completion within the day. He felt useful. He felt knowledgeable. He felt pretty darn good.

Six months in the job, he hit a wall—well, more of a high hurdle. He realized that, although he had been ticking off to-dos, no one seemed to notice. He had yet to receive a "good job" or "nice work on that project." And now, with his sensors on high alert, he noticed that every time he finished a task, no one said anything. *Not a thing.*

Doubt replayed in his brain like a bad tune. Am I doing the right thing? Do people think I'm good at my job? Do I know what I'm doing, or do I only *think* I know what I'm doing? It was driving him mad.

Panicked, he asked me for my opinion. I was working as a management consultant and coach at the time and thought myself qualified in these matters. In this situation, it actually wasn't my training as a coach that helped, but my own experience at work. I had recently started working for a new employer and was also feeling unnoticed—unloved, really. I asked a more seasoned co-worker what I should do about the situation and relayed the advice to my then-boyfriend/now-husband:

**No news is good news. If you haven't heard that you're doing a bad job, you're doing a good job.**

The wise veteran explained that managers are too busy to stop and give me a pat on the back every time I complete a project. I remember being shocked, thinking, "If they are my managers, isn't that their job—to give me feedback about my work?" I chuckle at my naïveté back then.

I explained it with a little more compassion to my husband. "You've just graduated," I advised. "And you are used to getting an 'A' for every project and piece of homework you turn in. It's not that way on the job. You need to trust that you are doing things right until your manager redirects your effort. And if you need feedback because you are not sure how to proceed, you are going to have to ask for it."

My husband wasn't alone. For more than fifteen years prior to entering the workforce, younger workers have grown accustomed to the grade-for-work exchange. We shouldn't blame them for expecting that agreement to continue into their professional lives. But beyond the needs of the newly graduated, the fact is that all employees need to know that they are good at their jobs in order to support a healthy sense of confidence. If you want happy employees, recognize their successes. Perhaps every worker deserves an "A" now and then.

—Brenda Kowske

# 4

# Exciting Work

**W**ILLIAM PULLED his hat down low to block the howling wind. Snowflakes toy with the idea of winter as they dust his work boots. He walks the yard faster; it's unseasonably cold even for Stockholm and his lighter jacket isn't providing the necessary warmth.

As the pale dawn breaks over the rail yard, steel glints out of the corner of his eye. Rail ties, stacked in seemingly random mountains, and boxcars slumber, each showing its age through rust and graffitied tattoos. The all-too-familiar rumble in the distance reminds him of the job to do today, a word of encouragement whispered by the trains every day for the past twenty years.

Once predictable, changes in the last decade have, at times, sent him spinning. The railroad was a hard-working and stable occupation. In his younger days, he took solace in the immovable rock that was the rail—as steady as a slow-moving locomotive chugging toward its destination.

Frankly, he didn't expect to have to be learning maintenance for new fuel technologies and increasingly complex logistics as he neared retirement. Like the high-speed rail, opportunities came flying his way—and sometimes passed him by in the blink of an eye. Not this time. Growing weary of the same logistical challenges—weather, line breakdowns, rail yard capacity issues—he hopped on the "green" movement and had not had time to look back. Acting as a liaison with the vendors selling the latest technology, it's William's job to make the different elements fit together and make the rail increasingly more efficient.

Smiling to himself, he shakes his head. What a wild ride. Occupationally speaking, he feels as though he's twenty again. At first a skeptic, he can't help but catch the "green" fever—his vendors' enthusiasm is infectious. While the fuddy-duddies he started his career with are groaning that "these new kids think they know everything," William has become a bridge between generations. What the railroad is offering today is good for riders, the company, Sweden, and the environment. It doesn't get more exciting than that.

While some assumed William might coast into retirement, he instead chose to reinvigorate his career. His path is actually pretty typical. The needs to feel engaged by work and to have autonomy to do work well are two issues that are voiced by employees all over the world. When we asked employees to define what they mean by "exciting work" they said they are looking for a chance to make a difference; being able to use their skills to the fullest extent possible; the latitude to exercise their leadership skills and problem-solving abilities; and the opportunity to learn something new.

"Exciting work" is a category perhaps best summed up by the comment, "I want a satisfying job that I look forward to spending each day doing." When we talk about work excitement, it taps into employees' feelings of intrinsic job satisfaction and interest in their work. It is the inner sense that we *want* to work, spurred on by challenging and exciting assignments.[1] Is that too much to ask? It turns out that 60 percent of employees globally become excited about their work, and that's good news for employers. The bad news is that there's another 40 percent who are not excited about the work they do.

## Is William Getting the Chance to Do Exciting Work?

William is lucky, relatively speaking, when it comes to his work. Eighty-four percent of Nordic European men over fifty working in the government or transportation sectors like their work—they're satisfied with it—and for 81 percent their work provides them with a feeling of personal accomplishment. That's the good news. But when we asked employees like William whether they were *excited* by their work, just 62 percent agreed, only slightly above the global average. People who said they wanted challenging and fulfilling work—in a nutshell, exciting work—made comments like:

- "To know that I make a difference"
- "A sense of accomplishment"
- "Interesting work"
- "Opportunities to excel and be challenged by the work I do"
- "I would like to broaden the scope of the work that I do, be a little more creative"
- "Use my knowledge effectively, not stick me into a pattern where I can't excel"
- "A challenging job, not the same every day with tasks I can do with my eyes closed"

How do those who are excited about work act? They are the ones who, when the alarm clock goes off, it's up and out of bed. They solve work problems while driving, shaving, or watching TV because it's fun to think about. They don't dread Mondays, and there's no sinking feeling in their gut when they open their work email. They are focused, active players in the organization's success. Clearly, not all employees (and their respective employers) are as fortunate.

# Finding Excitement at Work

For many, work is the same, day in and day out. From the earliest debates in the field of education at the turn of the 20th century, the thinkers of the day doubted that humans could be slotted in the rote tasks of the industrial age.[2] To not use your mind or skills, to be unable to fulfill the potential you know you possess, is a sure recipe for boredom at a minimum; even worse, it can lead to a pervasive melancholy or apathy about work. People need to be *challenged.*

Figure 4.1. Work Excitement by Global Industry

- Health Care Services
- Electronics Manufacturing
- Education
- Health Care Products/Pharma
- Construction/Engineering
- Banking Services
- Financial Services
- Global Average
- Heavy Manufacturing
- Business Services
- Food Industry
- Retail/Wholesale Trade
- Government
- Communication Services/Utilities
- Transportation Services
- Light Manufacturing

0%   10%   20%   30%   40%   50%   60%   70%   80%

**Percentage Favorable**

Some employees have the pleasure of being invigorated by their jobs, perhaps dealing with life-and-death situations or being at the cutting edge of innovation. Employees working in the top two industries for exciting work, health care services and electronics manufacturing, face these types of challenges (see Figure 4.1).

Consider the health care services industry. Excitement can certainly be found in healing the sick, helping patients fight for their lives, and responding to medical emergencies. Fulfillment can be found almost every day through the positive impact employees have on those under their care; this impact is often immediate and obvious. This is especially true for physicians and nurses. Our research clearly indicates that doctors' and nurses' work excitement scores outpace others working in the health care services industry, such as administrators and health aides.

Figure 4.2 reveals the global ranking of work excitement by major job type. Executives and managers are the most likely to find their work exciting, and by margins far exceeding those of workers in clerical jobs and those who work as operators and laborers. The autonomy in decision

**Figure 4.2. Work Excitement by Global Job Type**

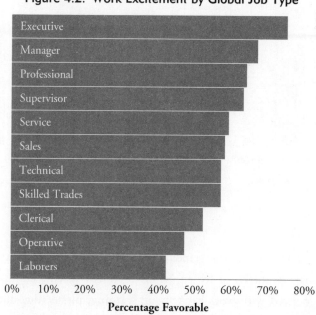

making that is granted on higher rungs of the career ladder certainly contributes to a greater sense of work excitement.

## What Makes Work Exciting

Regardless of industry or job, what are the catalysts for making work more exciting? We found five conditions of work that excited employees: (1) having been cross-trained, (2) working in R&D, (3) working in an expatriate assignment, (4) working remotely, and (5) working for a non-profit organization (NPO) (see Figure 4.3). The levels of work excitement for employees in these five circumstances exceed those of employees not working in such circumstances by a significant margin. For example, 70 percent of those who have been cross-trained were excited by their work, compared to only 52 percent who have not been cross-trained. That's quite a gap!

**Figure 4.3. Work Excitement Under Different Employment Conditions**

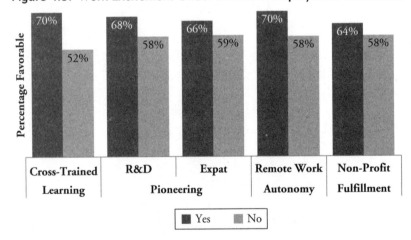

These work arrangements (cross-training; working in R&D, as an expat, remotely, or for an NPO) represent specific cultural conditions associated with work excitement: learning, pioneering, autonomy, and fulfillment, respectively.

Learning provides an opportunity to break out of daily work and try something new. The vast majority of employees who have opportunities to learn on the job say their work is exciting. Cross-training, as a talent management program, usually focuses on high-potential employees—those slotted for greatness. These employees are thrust into new departments, divisions, or processes for the purpose of developing an understanding of the *whole*. Employees who are cross-trained are forever changed; they can consider the impact of decisions down the line and across groups. This kind of learning elevates their thinking and significantly develops their ability to serve the organization. Indeed, learning a new skill can often bring with it a sense of hope and opportunity—a chance to do something different and perform at a higher level. Cross-training in particular is an effective tool for developing and motivating employees, as well as creating exciting work. Not only does it teach a new, broader perspective, but it also carries the rubber stamp of approval by employees' leaders, a sure sign of recognition that enables workers to break the monotony of a single job.

Pioneering, forging ahead and blazing new paths, can also provide a sense of excitement, an anticipation of diving into the unknown. We've highlighted two employment scenarios that characterize this experience, including working in the forefront of industry in an R&D function and working on the edges of the organization's geographical boundaries on an expatriate assignment. Working in R&D certainly embodies the spirit of pioneering. The job itself is constant trial of the new. Often fraught with more unsuccessful experiments than promising results, R&D employees experience first-hand the race to unveil the next innovation and problem solve in real time. Tweaking formulas and processes, trying new mediums and methods, all at breakneck speed, these employees are the workplace equivalent of adrenaline junkies. As they stand at the forefront of the unknown, at times they must go with their best guesses and take leaps of faith, sometimes with significant investment depending on their success or failure. Discovering and harnessing the new is exciting.

In most cases, employees on expat assignment are the cowboys of the business world; they are taming new markets, forging new alliances, and advancing the organization's frontier. Often, they've landed in a foreign country with a vastly different culture, but expats thrive on the new and adventurous. Not only are expats well-suited for pioneering, but they are also highly trusted by their leaders. These are people who can get things done despite the obstacles of working on the frontier far from home. It comes as no surprise that, in both cases, the majority of these pioneering employees (68 and 66 percent, respectively) find their work exciting.

Remote workers have a sense of independence—the thrill that comes with freedom. When employees work without a net, the onus is on them to make good decisions and act decisively. When success follows, it builds self-confidence. When an organization allows an employee to work from home, we can assume that leaders have abandoned a micro-managing style, at least in terms of hovering over an employee's cube wall making sure they are not logged into Facebook. Employees who work remotely enjoy a certain amount of independence. We've found that 70 percent of remote employees find their work exciting.

Working for an NPO can offer a mission-driven employment experience, and employees have told us that excitement translates into fulfillment: expending energy in a job that matters. Although for-profit organizations often have missions that benefit society, they are also driven by bottom-line financial goals. NPOs, of course, are typically targeted at improving society and allocate surplus funds to support their mission, not their shareholders. It's certainly not always the case, but many employees in NPOs represent a worker who is seeking to contribute to a greater good. Not surprisingly, 64 percent of those employees report that their work is exciting.

So what does exciting work mean to you and your employees? Being on the cutting edge of technology? Traveling? Learning to operate in a new culture? Embracing an element of risk or danger? Doing something bigger or grander than anyone has ever done before? Once you know the answer to the above, the question becomes: "How can you create it?"

# Why Exciting Work Matters to Your Business Success

Exciting work is fundamentally about having a satisfying job, a job that matches well with one's skills and abilities and provides a sense of accomplishment. If employees don't like the kind of work they do, don't expect them to be excited and enthusiastic about it.

*Job satisfaction* is the broader term and represents a summary of how employees feel about their jobs. We know job satisfaction is one of the best predictors of employee retention. Unless they have no alternatives, employees are not going to stay in jobs they don't like. Similar to our own research, Beverly Kay and Sharon Jordan-Evans list "exciting, challenging work" at the very top of their list of reasons why employees stay at their jobs, based on their independent survey of over fifteen thousand workers.[3]

In order for organizational managers to find out exactly what satisfies or dissatisfies employees, they need to talk with them. If employees are dissatisfied, it is crucial to understand the reasons because there's a clear link between job dissatisfaction and decreased commitment. Dissatisfaction is also an "expense" because it leads to higher employee turnover. Just as importantly, in our estimation, dissatisfied employees are not realizing their full potential—for themselves or for their employers.

# Influencing Job Satisfaction and Work Excitement the Right Way

There are a number of key contributors to job satisfaction and work excitement, but among the most important are

- *Clear expectations.* Setting realistic expectations is always important, particularly with new employees or when the nature of an existing position changes. Employees who experience job overload, excessive duties, and incompatible demands are more likely to be dissatisfied with their jobs.

- *Identification with work.* As with our discussion above regarding those working for NPOs, employees tend to be more satisfied when they identify with their work and see it as being central to who they are. Similarly, when employees clearly understand their organization's strategic direction—or value their organization's mission—they are more likely to contribute more of themselves to their work.

- *Sense of accomplishment.* When employees can see the results of their efforts, they are more satisfied. Generally, employees want to be efficient and productive and are frustrated when they are not. Also, employees who work on the "whole" product or service have a greater sense of accomplishment than those who only work on a part of a product or service.

- *Responsibility.* When employees feel responsible for their work, including being able to make decisions, it improves job satisfaction.

- *Feedback and recognition.* Employees should be told the extent to which they are doing their jobs correctly and effectively. Feedback reinforces what people do well and helps them improve—and that just feels good.

# How to Diagnose Your Organization's State of Job Satisfaction and Work Excitement

Organizations with employees who are not excited, enthusiastic, and satisfied with their work are at a distinct competitive disadvantage, and diagnosing the causes of dissatisfaction is a critical step. Of course, some reasons for job dissatisfaction may be beyond the control of an immediate manager, but managers still need to work at minimizing any problems.

Some questions for managers to ask themselves and their teams include:

- To what extent are employees able to charge ahead and do what they do best?
- Are current job assignments challenging? Do they fully utilize employee skills and abilities?

- What stands in the way of employees doing their work? More precisely, do changing priorities, limited resources, and poor fit of employees to jobs represent obstacles to performance? What barriers are the most frustrating to employees?
- Can employees see the impact of their work? Do they get a sense of accomplishment from completing projects?
- When employees enter an organization or work unit, do they have a realistic understanding of the job expectations? Do managers have a realistic understanding of employee expectations for specific jobs?
- Do managers have good working relationships with subordinates? Are they readily available? Do managers motivate and challenge employees? Do managers reward outstanding performance? Do managers make sure employees are properly trained and equipped to do their jobs?

# Guiding Principles to Foster Job Satisfaction and Work Excitement

Specific steps to improve work excitement and job satisfaction will depend on answers to the questions outlined above and others relevant to your situation. Even so, some basic principles underlie any effective action.

## Job Fit

People's skills, interests, and abilities should match their job requirements. Being in a job where you are ill-suited and ill-prepared can be intimidating, frustrating, and demoralizing. Managers should take great care in placing people in jobs they will find challenging. This might be easier said than done and may even mean moving employees out of one group and into another.

In order to get the most of employees when it comes to commitment, values, or ideas, Po Branson, in his book *What Should I Do with My Life?*, suggests not just benefits, incentives, and education, but finding the work that employees are most passionate about. He states, "We need to encourage people to find their sweet spot. Productivity explodes when people love what they do."[4]

Managers should also pay attention to "expectation management." Realistically portraying what is expected from an employee as well as the environment in which the work is performed will ultimately improve job satisfaction and good-will toward the company. Violated expectations or broken "psychological contracts" tend to cause disillusionment, frustration, and cynicism.

At Bailard, Inc., a private investment firm based in the San Francisco Bay area, the average employee tenure is thirteen years, thanks to a culture that places a high value on trust, employee development, and exciting work. With open communication, junior staffers feel safe to bring up new ideas, ask questions of senior employees, and initiate projects in business areas most interesting to them. Matt Johnson, a vice president of Bailard's health care investments, started out as an entry-level investment associate in 2001, ultimately working in every department. Johnson was able to find an area within the firm that was particularly interesting to him—a perfect job fit—and began working more intensely in that area. "You really feel like you have a hand in the day-to-day operation," says Johnson.[5]

## Leadership and Management

It is part of a manager's job to understand what motivates employees—what they like and don't like about their work. Simply discussing with employees what really excites them can be a significant first step in improving their satisfaction.

At Millennium Pharmaceuticals they have found that exciting work often comes in the form of simply keeping the entrepreneurial spirit alive. When Mark Levin was CEO, each month he and his team leaders got together to brainstorm, reigniting the "passion and fanaticism" they used to have when the company was so small everyone could fit around one table. By giving each group a chance to discuss and come up with new ideas, leaders and employees walked away enthusiastic about their jobs and their company.[6]

Managers also need to be on the lookout for trends that suggest dissatisfaction so that steps can be taken at the first sign of trouble. Pay particular attention to individual withdrawal in the form of tardiness, absenteeism, and doing fewer of the extra things. Also, changes in management, large-scale organizational changes, and unrealized promotions can lead to a diminished sense of work excitement.

Changes that are the result of a downturn in business provide special challenges for organizations. Difficult economic conditions spurred the iconic company Radio Flyer to outsource its manufacturing to China and to lay off about half of its Chicago-based workforce. In the aftermath, Robert Pasin, CEO and grandson of the company founder, created a fun and dynamic workplace where employees were involved in decision making. By pulling together in teams and committees to oversee various elements in the workplace, employees felt like "part of the team" and that their ideas counted. As an example, the wellness committee created a benefit through which employees are reimbursed up to $300 annually for health-related activities such as running marathons or receiving counseling for weight loss. Still another group of employees interested in environmental issues launched an initiative to reduce the carbon footprint of the company and of employee homes.[7]

## Job Design

As a general practice, managers should seek ways to enrich jobs by building in and reinforcing variety, autonomy, feedback, significance, and accomplishment. Enabling people to use all their skills and creativity to get things done is a sure-fire path to creating more exciting work and higher levels of satisfaction with the work itself.

This is exactly what American Express recently did in its call center operations. With a vision "to become the world's most respected service brand," the company discovered that the quality of its customer service depends heavily on the level of engagement and empowerment of its call center workers. "Customer care professionals" have done away with the scripts and blazed a new model for handling customer service calls, which the company refers to as "Relationship Care." This new strategy allows the customer care professional to think independently and make autonomous and quick decisions to help customers. For example, customer care professionals can set up conference calls to try to resolve disputes between customers and vendors. Relationship Care was rolled out in conjunction with improved recruiting, upgraded training, more career options, and a more sophisticated pay-for-performance system. As employees are continually assessed by customer feedback, they can self-correct mistakes, improving relationships with customers and the quality of service. By empowering its employees, American Express operates at a more engaged level, resulting in more engaged customers.[8]

Consider also the example of Harrah's Entertainment, Inc., the world's largest provider of branded casino entertainment. At Harrah's, employees feel engaged and appreciated because they are encouraged to communicate regularly with management about their personal and on-the-job needs. For instance, at one property, workers asked to shift work schedules to fit in better with their daily lives, and management adopted the change. In addition, Harrah's now provides Internet access so employees can stay in touch with their families while at work. Local, plugged-in leadership helps enhance the work experience for its workers.[9]

# Concrete Actions to Improve Job Satisfaction and Work Excitement

Different workplaces have different needs, but there are four basic steps any manager can take to kick-start job satisfaction:

- *Conduct realistic job previews*. As the name suggests, this involves presenting prospective employees with both positive and negative information about the job. This shows integrity. It also builds a sense of confidence and trust on the part of job applicants toward the hiring manager. Realistic job previews are also an effective tool for communicating general performance expectations, the nature of the work, and the conditions under which that work is to be performed.

This is an area where Harrah's Entertainment is also doing it right. After an extensive recruiting process, new hires go through a special orientation and training program that not only covers the expectations the company has of them in their new roles, but also what they can expect from the company. During orientation, it is made clear that the company has a responsibility to get to know employees and their talents so that everyone can work more efficiently, using role models and leaders and the right resources and tools to do their jobs. Expectations are set in an environment in which praise and recognition are expressed and new goals are regularly set.[10]

- **Participate with employees individually and in groups to understand why they feel the way they do.** If you are a high-level manager, set up a process to touch base with employees who report to your direct reports. Find out what is working and what isn't for these employees, especially as it relates to the work they do and their excitement about the work itself. Benefits accrue for managers who follow this counsel. Not only will they learn more about the capabilities and interests of employees, but they'll hear ideas about new and innovative products and services, create a smoother operation, and develop a more satisfied workforce.

A variant of this recommendation is what happens at Eisai Company, a Japanese pharmaceutical maker. The company creates exciting and engaging work for its employees by using "innovation communities," a group of employees who span the company to work together on new products, services, or business processes. For Eisai, this means that every employee worldwide, regardless of title or function, participates in a health care–related project, such as investigating new structures and sizes of medicines that are more patient-friendly or creating social programs for families of

victims of Alzheimer's disease. The company believes it is important to show employees the people for whom the company designs
medicines so that the employees can see and understand what
issues patients find most significant. It's an incredibly successful
motivating tool as well.[11]

- ***Recognize employees for a job well done***. As we pointed out in
  Chapter 3, it is crucial to let people know when you appreciate
  their good work. This does not require a financial reward. Simply
  saying "thank you" can be both powerful and low cost.

- ***Remember to have fun***. Some of us grow up to conduct our business affairs with incredible seriousness. "No time for nonsense"
  is our mantra. But social activities such as team luncheons can
  go a long way toward building and maintaining strong working
  relationships. They not only give people a chance to interact on a
  more personal level, but they also provide a little fun and variety
  to a typical day's work.

  Zappos.com, an online retailer, uses unconventional means for
  keeping employees engaged and energetic about their work. The
  retailer's culture centers around ten values, including "Create
  fun and a little weirdness" and "Deliver WOW through service." Employees' performance reviews are heavily based on how
  employees perform against these values. One high-level example
  of fun involves a group of executives who work in "monkey row,"
  an area decorated in green foliage hanging from the ceiling.[12]

# 5

# Security of Employment

**H**ENRY'S WEEKLY CALL to the Singapore site is not going to go well. He's calling in from home because it's just too early to be in the office, and he also wants to somehow contain the bad news. He navigates the seemingly insane multiple-hurdle process of dialing into the teleconference and finds that the Singaporean management team is already on, making the usual small talk as Henry patiently waits.

The formalities of this group sometime drive him crazy, but today, given the tough message he has to deliver, he welcomes this moment to gather his thoughts. Finally, he begins the task at hand rather stiffly. "As you all know, we have suffered quarter-over-quarter losses in the Pharma group," he says. "The back-to-back recalls of Q1 and Q2 have shaken investor and consumer confidence. Our market share has shrunk in this sector, and corrective action is now critical." Henry forges ahead, purposely driving through the heavy silence on the line. "To your credit, the Singapore site has implemented higher yield and cost-saving measures, but in this climate those measures are simply not enough. Corporate needs you to cut 10 percent of the Singapore-based workforce by the end of the fiscal year. We're cutting back at headquarters too—10 percent."

As Henry expected, there's a long silence. He waits. Rajan, the site director, speaks first. "This is unfortunate news indeed," he laments quietly. "Our site has banded together during these difficult times and we agreed on tough choices. The employees have already been hit hard by past corrective actions, but they have held together and remained surprisingly loyal. Henry, this is going to be difficult to execute without impacting our production quotas, and the hit to employee morale will be [he pauses to contain his anxiety] *significant.*"

The second in command, Wong, weighs in quietly, "They just started to believe that the layoffs were over." Henry can relate. In fact, even though he's the one who was assigned to deliver the bad news to Singapore, he half thinks he could lose his own job once headquarters starts its cuts.

"I understand," says Henry. "But we can't ignore the drop in demand and what Wall Street is telling us. I will need a reduction-in-force plan by the end of the month. Your HR group should be consulted. Any questions?"

Silence.

"Okay. Then thank you, in advance, for the tough decisions you'll have to make in the coming months. The goal is to emerge a stronger, more agile organization, and these actions will have played no small role. We appreciate your help and commitment."

A few beeps indicating hang-ups on the other end of the line and it's over. Henry knows this is just the beginning of hard conversations with the Singapore group. In the back of his mind, doubt creeps forward. Maybe the purpose of the downsizing efforts are to improve company balance sheets and make the organization more attractive to potential buyers? That rumor has been circulating for months. Henry worries. Could he really be let go as well?

# What Makes Employees Feel Secure in Their Jobs?

Security is a fundamental human need, and people look for it in their work lives as much as they do in their personal lives. Dating back to psychology's early attempts at categorizing human needs and motivation, safety and security ranked right above eating, sleeping, and procreating.[1] Think about security as the opposite of insecurity, defined as, "the lack of confidence or assurance" (www.dictionary.com). Yes, employee confidence will likely be shaken if layoffs are looming, but feeling secure in one's job is more than that. Do you feel confident at work? Do you know all the faces at your office and who to ask for help to get things done? Is it largely easy and effortless? Is it *comfortable*?

Feelings of job insecurity have nasty effects on employees. Those feeling insecure also have poor job attitudes, a lower sense of involvement in their work, and decreased commitment to and trust in the organization. These employees are also more likely to think about quitting.[2] And let's not ignore the biggest issue: at a time when leaders need a lean workforce to work harder, insecure employees actually work less.[3] In 2010, 61 percent of employees worldwide rated their company as good or very good in providing job security, and 66 percent felt that they would not be laid off from their jobs. The remaining 34 percent are vulnerable to job insecurity fallout. Employees who said that security was the most important thing they wanted from their organizations want things such as:

- "A permanent job"
- "Job security"
- "Stability"
- "A safe, low-stress workplace"
- "Steady work"
- "Not be laid off and have hours cut back"
- "The ability to continue working in the present position"
- "I want the assurance that I have job security and will not be in a position of having my job eliminated to balance budget problems"

- "The best guarantee possible that my job will still be there one year from now"
- "Ways to cut costs without laying off workers"
- "Job security and not the threat of moving work to low-cost countries irrespective of quality or skills"

At its core, feeling secure is about trust: trusting oneself and trusting the environment. People at work tend to ask, first, can they trust themselves to do a good job? The answer to this question is partially related to the person's self-esteem or self-confidence; those who have higher self-esteem perceive more job security.[4] It also speaks to a match between job skills and performance expectations. Managers can allay this concern by making sure people are properly suited for their jobs, providing training opportunities, and recognizing people's successes.

Second, employees need to trust their leaders, specifically to provide continued employment.[5] There's no way around it: layoffs raise feelings of job insecurity.[6] Consider this: among employees whose organizations have downsized in the past twelve months, 51 percent rate their organizations as good or very good in providing job security. However, if no layoffs had occurred, 71 percent rate favorably the organization's commitment to job security.

As we look across the globe, it is clear that in this year of slow recovery from the Great Recession organizations utilized downsizing as a cost-saving measure to varying degrees (see Figure 5.1). Only slightly more than a quarter (28 percent) of employees in Japan and France reported layoffs. Except for Russian workers, employees in the other BRIC growth economies of Brazil, India, and China also witnessed fewer reductions in force.

Far more employees working in Russia (56 percent) have witnessed layoffs. The United States, the United Kingdom, and Canada also all rank above the global average in layoff frequency. What is the upshot? In these countries, leaders will need to rebuild trust in management.

**Figure 5.1. Country Ranking on Organizational Layoffs Within Last Twelve Months**

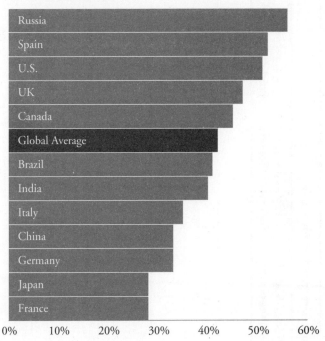

Essentially, employees' trust in the organization's leadership and management is under consideration, and this is a complicated issue. Globally, only half (51 percent) of employees trust their senior leaders.

# Building Trust

To build trust, past research shows that managers need to be seen as skilled and competent, benevolent, and ethical.[7] Our own research corroborates what previous research states. In fact, when we analyzed the top ten drivers of job security, we saw the themes of competence, benevolence, and ethics shine through (see Table 5.1). Employees trust competent leaders—those who lead an organization well, create work excitement, and compel the actions of others through a motivating vision

Table 5.1. Global Employee Ratings of the Drivers of Job Security

*Percent of employees responding favorably*

| Driver of Job Security | | Global Average | Senior/Middle Management | Professional/ Technical Workers | Service/ Production Workers |
|---|---|---|---|---|---|
| **Competence** | Well-led organization | 50% | 62% | 49% | 45% |
| | Work excitement | 60% | 71% | 63% | 53% |
| | Motivating vision | 47% | 62% | 45% | 40% |
| **Benevolence** | Career goal achievement | 52% | 67% | 53% | 43% |
| | Work/life balance support | 55% | 64% | 56% | 47% |
| | Safety is a priority | 63% | 71% | 61% | 61% |
| | Opportunity for development | 53% | 68% | 55% | 45% |
| | Opportunity to develop skills | 54% | 65% | 57% | 46% |
| **Ethics** | Contribution is valued | 55% | 68% | 55% | 48% |
| | CSR improves satisfaction | 51% | 62% | 50% | 46% |

of the future. Trust is built through benevolent actions, specifically by supporting employees' career goals, prioritizing safety at work, giving employees opportunities for development and growth, and developing employees' skills for the future. Finally, trustworthy leaders are ethical leaders. They give credit where credit is due by valuing the contributions of others and, through balancing multiple stakeholders' needs, they improve employee job satisfaction by investing time and resources in corporate social responsibility (CSR) efforts.

Employees are not going to feel secure unless their future holds promise. Who would feel secure on a sinking ship? Employees need to believe that the leadership team is competent, because this means the company will be able to provide jobs over the long term.

Employees have a fundamental desire to be appreciated and valued by their employers. Employees think to themselves: "If the organization is investing in me, it must want to keep me around." They look for signs that leaders care about them and want them to do well in their careers.

At the heart of trust lies the belief that the other person—the boss—will do the right thing and look out for employee interests. It is impossible to trust someone who lies or operates underhandedly. It seems obvious, but it's worth being crystal clear about it: employees want to work for ethical organizations and for leaders with integrity.[8]

Looking again at Table 5.1, the global average of each driver of job security shows us some areas of strength upon which trust can be built and other areas for development. Relatively speaking, more employees feel that safety is a priority (63 percent) and feel excited at work (60 percent). These are cornerstones that leaders can build upon. On the other hand, leaders have work to do in conveying a motivating vision of the future. At only 47 percent, the view of the future for most employees is murky and, therefore, employees will have a difficult time committing to the work and to the organization. With an unclear future, employees have little about which to feel secure.

Within various job roles, employees' perceptions are consistent on the drivers of job security. It comes as no surprise that senior leaders and middle managers score highest on these drivers. They are closer to the decisions being made and have a broader perspective. They are more likely to trust that their decisions are in the best interests of the company. Leaders and managers have a greater feeling of participation and control of the outcome.

In the middle, professional and technical individual contributors see more room for improvement, especially in the areas of competence: generally, only half feel their organization is well led (49 percent) and only 45 percent report that senior leaders have provided a motivating vision for them.

People who work in lower-level production and service jobs came in with the lowest ratings, with only 60 percent reporting that their companies provide job security for "people like themselves." That means that, on any given day, two of every five employees feel some degree of job insecurity. From this vantage point, the picture of trust and security is bleak. Scores on eight of the ten drivers of job security are less than 50 percent favorable, with areas for improvement in delivering a motivating vision (40 percent) and fostering a belief that employees can achieve their career goals within the organization (43 percent). Both of these areas are related to providing a stronger, more concrete vision of the future for production and service employees, as well as for the organization at-large.

The drivers of job security provide a roadmap of what organizations can do to enhance employee perceptions of job security. Using the three leadership themes of competence, benevolence, and ethics as the organizing framework, Table 5.2 re-states the conditions that cause employees to feel more secure in their jobs and outlines the organizational, leadership, and managerial requirements for building employee trust in the organization's future.

## The State of Job Insecurity

When we went to press in 2011, levels of unemployment in many Western economies remained high. Even organizations that were historically safe havens were facing difficult circumstances. In the United States, where

**Table 5.2. Driving Job Security Through Building Trust**

| | Employees feel more secure in their jobs when they: | Employee trust is strengthened by: |
|---|---|---|
| **Competent** | Believe that their organization is well-led and managed | Effective organizational design and leadership |
| | Are excited about their work | Management ensuring an effective job/person match |
| | Are motivated by the organization's vision of the future | Effective strategy combined with good communication skills |
| | Can achieve their career goals at their current organization | Career paths and aligned development goals |
| **Benevolent** | Feel that their efforts to balance work and personal responsibilities are supported | Management accommodating personal needs whenever possible |
| | See safety prioritized | Well-conceived safety plans and compliance, and communication about the value of safety |
| | Have opportunities for growth and development | Organizational growth coupled with effective talent management systems |
| | Get help in developing the skills they will need for the future | Clear career paths and supportive managers who clear obstacles to learning |
| **Ethical** | Believe that their contribution is valued by senior management | Recognition programs with senior management support and visibility |
| | Can personally relate to the organization's corporate social responsibility efforts | Employee involvement in CSR agenda planning and execution |

working for the government was once considered stable and secure employment, federal, state, or city workers were facing the grim result of gaping budget cuts. In 2010, at least twenty-six states cut jobs, with some implementing temporary layoffs. According to our latest tally, at least ninety-five thousand state and local government jobs were cut in the first half of 2010. Understandably, government employees—from firefighters to accountants—remain intensely concerned about future layoffs and job security. In just one poignant example, newly graduated teachers in California, who were once told, "There's a huge need for teachers," are vying with twenty-six thousand recently laid off teachers for thirty-nine spots in the state.[9]

Even as the economy slowly rebounds, major impediments to employment and job security remain. As the Department of Labor reported in the summer of 2009, the jobless rate in the United States was 9.5 percent and nearly fifteen million Americans were looking for work.[10] Companies were flooded with applicants, but many positions remained unfilled because applicant skills were not matched with job requirements. Mobility is critical to a healthy job market, but homeowners found themselves locked in place because of an ailing real-estate market.

While consumer spending rose slightly in August 2010 compared to a year earlier, consumer savings were up even more, reflecting caution about the economy and job security. Without a rise in consumer spending and an ability to place skilled workers in open positions, economic growth suffers.[11]

To be sure, the impact of the economy on job security has touched all sectors and has exposed many weak points in employee job security. These four stories, as originally told by *The Wall Street Journal*, highlight both the impact of job insecurity and the resilience and determination of today's workforce.

1.  Job seekers such as Paul Hansen, fifty-two, a former vice president and director of accounting for Hensley Beverage Co. in Phoenix, Arizona, spent eighteen months searching for a job. After sending out hundreds of resumes for controller or financial director

positions, he received two offers. For Hansen, the first few months of unemployment were a welcome reprieve; however, as the months rolled on, his frustration grew. Hansen cut back on household expenses and found himself living off his severance package and unemployment benefits. While unemployed, he took care of his newborn granddaughter, volunteered for a literacy group, and did more work around the house. To relieve stress he went to the gym an hour every day. Meanwhile, Hansen had five recruiters helping him, which kept him motivated and persistent in finding a job. Hansen feels that not earning his Certified Public Accountant credential may have hurt his chances with prospective employers. Because Hansen had worked for Hensley Beverage for twenty-three years, the promotions he received led to a false sense of security that the CPA credential would not be necessary.[12]

2. After seventeen months, Bill Jacobs finally found a job that offered him his old pay, but it was something completely different from what he was doing previously. Jacobs, an IT engineer, who was originally featured in a *Wall Street Journal* story about long-term employment, initially did volunteer work with patients with Alzheimer's disease and depression. Although unpaid, the job gave Jacobs a sense of worth. He was able to stay afloat for a while thanks to unemployment checks, a hefty savings emergency fund, his wife's job, and taking on costly home repairs himself. Jacobs found his current job by playing Christmas songs on his trumpet on the streets of Chicago. He realized he could make about $15 an hour for two hours of playing. A side benefit was that it also improved his attitude. He followed up at a casino, where he had previously dropped off his resume for an IT position, but this time inquired about an opening for a musician. Now he plays his music at the same pay he had at his IT job.[13]

3. Mary Lou Belmont, fifty-six, from St. Augustine, Florida, has been without full-time work since November 2008, when she

lost her job as a compliance manager with GMAC Home Services LLC. Since then Belmont and her husband—whose spray-foam-insulation business failed during the real-estate bust—accumulated more than $100,000 in debt from credit cards and a home-equity credit line. To make ends meet, the Belmonts' parents helped with cash. She eventually found part-time work that pays slightly above minimum wage. Belmont and her husband are willing to live apart if she can find a job outside northeast Florida, but their mobility is hampered by their mortgage. Their five-bedroom, five-bathroom home is on the market for $929,000, and potential buyers are scarce. On the positive side, Belmont has been offered an administrative job, but it is less than half her previous $117,000 salary.[14]

4. Tony Estrada, sixty, a Peruvian emigrant who has lived in the United States for more than thirty years, has been out of work for more than two years. Estrada is considering something he never thought he'd do: moving in with his parents. A former employee of Lowe's warehouse in Riverside County, California, Estrada experienced a negative domino effect after surgery for prostate cancer in August 2007. The surgery was covered by health insurance, but when he was ready to go back to work in April 2008, he learned he was away longer than the twelve weeks of unpaid leave guaranteed by the federal Family and Medical Leave Act. Originally his boss said he'd be eligible to come back in six months, but the economy continued to worsen and Estrada remained unemployed. After his unemployment benefits ran out, he asked his auto dealer to take back his Mazda 6, as he could no longer afford the payments. He could stay with friends, but only if he could pay rent. His children had no room for him at their homes. If Estrada cannot find a job, his plan of last resort is to stay with his parents—who relocated to Puerto Rico to be closer to the United States—until he's eligible for Social Security at

age sixty-two. These days Estrada questions whether the United States really is the strongest country in the world. "I guess I was wrong," he said.[15]

# How to Diagnose Employees' Current State of Job Security

Offering job security solutions to employers is no easy task given how many outside variables are at play. For-profit organizations must make decisions about employment levels based on factors like customer demand, cost structures, profit objectives, corporate values, and underlying economic conditions. Non-profit organizations also face pressure on staffing levels based on contributions, episodic donations, and grants, all of which are influenced by general economic conditions.

Diagnosing an organization's state of job security means that managers have to figure out exactly how employees feel about their jobs and the health and well-being of the enterprise. In short, managers need to stay connected to their employee base; they need to ask questions and listen to what employees say. This is especially true in difficult economic times. Not only will staying connected inform management, but it will also instill a sense of security, cohesiveness, and knowledge in the workforce. It's essential for employees to hear that they are working toward a result and not just spinning their wheels.

# Guiding Principles and Concrete Actions Organizations Can Take to Create Job Security

Economies operate in cycles. Periods of brutal economic and employment conditions are typically followed by periods of growth, recruitment, and hiring. Regardless of these cycles, or perhaps because of such cycles, we believe there are four fundamental things organizations can do to create a feeling of security for their employees.

## Clarify the Employment Proposition

What is the organization's commitment to its workforce when the market for its products and services declines? Wayne Cascio[16,17] has argued convincingly about the negative financial long-term impact of corporate downsizing; he finds no evidence of improved financial performance for companies that conduct large-scale layoffs. In reality, companies that downsized significantly underperformed in terms of profit margin, return on investment, return on equity, market-to-book ratio, and industry-adjusted total return on common stock compared to companies that did not downsize. Overall layoff announcements also have a negative impact on stock-market prices. Cascio also argues that learning- or knowledge-based organizations that downsize are at risk of losing large pieces of organizational memory that can also lead to decreased financial performance. One caveat: although stable organizations that avoided layoffs showed the best financial performance, those that conducted targeted layoffs accompanied by asset restructuring fared slightly better than companies that conducted indiscriminate downsizing. In sum, downsizing will not lead to increased profitability unless it is part of a broader business plan.

Our own research shows a negative impact on employee engagement when a company downsizes in response to a downturn in business. In organizations that have downsized in the past twelve months, employees report an Employee Engagement Index (EEI) score of 52 percent. As we explained in Chapter 2, the EEI is the average percentage of employees who agreed with the four items in the index that measure: pride, satisfaction, advocacy, and commitment. Figure 5.2 indicates that employees who have not witnessed layoffs fare much better, with an EEI score of 63 percent. That eleven point difference in the EEI is statistically significant, clearly demonstrating the negative effect of layoffs on employee motivation and commitment at work.

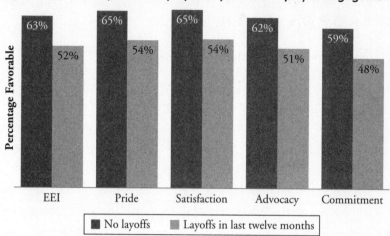

Figure 5.2. The Impact of Employee Layoffs on Employee Engagement

A very clear example of an employment proposition can be found at Lincoln Electric in Cleveland, Ohio, where a guaranteed-employment contract has become a hallmark of the business.

## Share Information Openly

Companies can cultivate an incredible amount of employee good-will when they go to unusual lengths to maintain job security for their employees. Consider the experience of Anthony Wilder Design/Build Inc., a residential architecture and construction company based in Maryland, founded by husband-and-wife team Anthony and Elizabeth Wilder. The Wilders openly share company financial results with their employees. They use an open-book management strategy that seeks to help employees to think and act like owners. This high level of transparency may just be what allowed most employees to keep their jobs in 2008—a troublesome economic year for most in that industry. In the fall of 2008, when the economy took a nosedive, senior management asked employees to take pay cuts, and most employees lost 20 to 30 percent

## SIDEBAR: A MODEL EMPLOYMENT PROPOSITION

### Guaranteed Employment at Lincoln Electric

Lincoln Electric, with global headquarters in Cleveland, Ohio, is the world's largest manufacturer of electric arc welding machinery. Employing 9,300 employees across twenty countries, the company is a technological leader in the global welding industry. Deeply embedded in Lincoln Electric's culture is a long-term commitment to job security. Even in the midst of a recession, 2008 marked sixty years without layoffs. In fact, Lincoln Electric is a pioneer in leading a high-performance culture, where for decades employees have been viewed as assets. At Lincoln it is considered good business to take care of employees.

Founded in 1895 by John Lincoln, an inventor who was enthralled with electricity, the company first focused on the development of electric vehicles. In the early 1900s when the gas-engine car became prevalent, Lincoln successfully shifted the company's focus to include steel welding. In 1914, John's brother, James, took over leadership of the company. The Lincoln brothers, sons of a preacher, both highly valued hard work and shared a strong religious perspective. They believed that providing steady employment and a high amount of respect was a Christian value and also a necessity for the company's financial success.

In 1958, Lincoln Electric instituted a Guaranteed Continuous Employment Plan, a no-layoff policy that has remained in place since then. The policy covers Cleveland employees who have worked for three or more years and who complete their daily responsibilities and meet performance expectations. These employees are guaranteed at least thirty hours of work each week. However, the company reserves the right to change an employee's job and responsibilities as well as his or her pay rate. Written into the policy is the option for the company to break its guarantee of continuous employment if conditions such as recessions or national disasters beyond its control jeopardize the company's survival.

With the recent recession in 2008, management held to their employment guarantee, but reduced hours to thirty or thirty-two a week for most employees. The reduced hours resulted in a 35 percent payroll reduction, but there were no layoffs. Management views this ability to reduce hours as a highly effective tool for managing costs while maintaining its employment guarantee.

Lincoln Electric's growth, steady profits, and international presence is a testament to the success of the employment guarantee. The benefits of the company's no layoff policy include a highly flexible workforce that adapts easily to new positions and departments. The resulting workforce stability also ensures that company-specific knowledge is retained and severance costs and future recruiting and training expenses are spared. The policy has successfully encouraged employees to increase their productivity and work for the better of the company. In addition, Lincoln Electric has remained union-free since its inception.[18]

of their salaries. The Wilders went one step further, taking a 50 percent cut. The Wilders' action helped employees feel committed, and their sacrifice paid off. In 2009 the company gave out back pay for the months since the cut.

At Wilder employees work harder to keep costs low, knowing that every dollar spent impacts the bottom line, their incomes, and ultimately the security of their jobs. By staying open about company finances, Anthony Wilder Design/Build Inc. managed to retain all but two employees during the economic downturn—both of whom they'd like to offer their jobs back to someday.[19]

## Prepare Employees for Current and Future Opportunities

As our research shows, organizations that invest more in employee training and development tend to outperform those that invest less (see Chapter 2). Commitment levels at these companies are also much stronger. Employees are acutely aware of the realities of the marketplace and how quickly circumstances can change, so they appreciate companies that help them prepare for the future and build their skill base.

Caterpillar offers a case in point. In a shaky economy, sometimes nothing is more important when considering a new position than job security. For Miguel Ortegon, the decision to accept a position with Caterpillar Inc. was made easier when he learned that Caterpillar would put him through a nine-week training program at a local community college. This led to his feeling the company was vested in his future with them.[20]

## Be Flexible and Create Flexibility for Employees

Creating a dynamic workplace in which employees don't feel chained to a specific task or even a specific physical space can create a greater sense of security, engagement, and commitment.

At Deloitte, a tax, auditing, and consulting services corporation that employs more than forty-five thousand, accountants are able to choose the focus for their work, whether tax or auditing. This allows employees to be more selective with their clients and their time and also makes the job working-mother friendly. The latter point has become particularly important as Deloitte's demand for women in management has skyrocketed. Deloitte's "career customization program" allows employees to ramp up or slow down based on where they are in their careers and lives. The flexibility also gives working moms the chance to maintain their certifications or licenses and stay current in the field. By staying professionally active through continuing education, accountants are able to enhance their resumes, stay relevant in this fast-changing field, and safeguard their jobs.[21]

# 6

# Pay

**CHEN LEI SITS** at his desk, staring at his screen. The Lunar New Year holiday is right around the corner and it will be a welcome break from the grind of retail. As a buyer for the largest regional supermarket in China's Pearl River Delta, things move at a breakneck pace for Chen. He's feeling as though his neck is about to snap from sitting hunched over, his face eight inches from the screen; the holiday couldn't come at a better time. He hopes the Year of the Rabbit lives up to the hype and brings respite after the ferocity synonymous with the Year of the Tiger. He'd rather be hiding in a burrow than chasing his tail.

Chen takes off his glasses and leans back in his faux-leather office chair. It's time for a change. It's nothing but tunnel vision at his job, a singular focus on the immediate task. Oh sure, there's innuendo about "growth" and "advancement," but it's been nine months and he hasn't seen any indication that the hype is anything more than wishful thinking.

"Why bother spending my energy on training when I can just get a new job that pays more?" It's a long climb to the top, or a short hop to a higher salary—a no-brainer. He smirks to himself. His parents can't understand moving jobs every year. Whenever his latest career plans come up in conversation, they look at him as if he's crazy. They'll never understand. They worked their fingers to the bone in factories, building up this industrial region. They had no options and no choices. In order to make any semblance of a livable wage, they were destined to work dawn until dusk—or later.

Boy, how the tides have turned. Long, *long* gone are the days of worker loyalty, thankfulness, and obedience—at least Chen and his colleagues think so. Management is scrambling to keep younger employees like him, betting the bank that the New Year bonus—the thirteen-month salary—will entice him to stay. It's true. If it's enough, Chen Lei might consider staying, but what is "enough" when you can always get more by moving?

# The Pay-for-Work Exchange

Chen faces a happy problem that only the lucky have to solve. He benefits from what economists and industrialists fear—a labor shortage. This is especially true in the manufacturing sector in China. The situation is drastically different for employees in the Western nations in production, service, and knowledge sectors alike. Higher-than-average levels of unemployment push worker supply up and incomes down. But regardless of situation and circumstance, a fundamental truth remains—we all work for money.

Clearly, we don't work *only* for money, but the pay-for-work exchange is the foundation of the employer-employee agreement. It serves as our motivation to come to work, but does it spur us to work hard? In this day and age, it is the medium by which people acquire their basic needs, and therefore a basic need in and of itself.[1] Twenty-five percent of employees globally stated that fair compensation was the most important thing they wanted from their organizations. Below is a sampling of their actual comments:

- "Fair pay for the work I do"
- "Compensation that is fair and respect(ful)"
- "Unfreeze pay"
- "A high salary"
- "Good pay for a hard day's work"
- "Fair cost-of-living increases"
- "A decent pay rate and affordable benefits"
- "Honest pay for an honest day's work"
- "To be paid competitively and recognized for the work I do"
- "A raise—it's been three years"

These are feelings we've all had about our pay at one point or another: pay needs to be fair and it needs to be *enough*. Comments about raises also appear frequently. In 2010, 13 percent of U.S. organizations froze merit and cost-of-living increases.[2] For companies that kept them, they were likely to be 2- to 3-percent increases, with an average of 2.7 percent[3]—about the same rate as the 2.6 percent change in cost-of-living, or the Consumer Price Index, from January 2009 to January 2010. Employees are stating clearly that they expect a salary "thaw," and increases should track with inflation as living continues to become more expensive. With that said, the projected raise for 2011 is expected to outstrip inflation; with only 2 percent of U.S. organizations expecting to freeze salaries in 2011, organizations project an average raise of 2.9 percent, but the annual change in the CPI was only 1.6 percent from January 2010 to 2011. If organizations are planning to give raises that on average exceed the cost of living, then giving a raise must mean more to employees than simply putting bread on the table.

Beyond the black-and-white needs fulfilled by pay raises, there is an emotional component. Raises play an important role in signaling to employees that they are valued and important, and that their work matters. Employees are telling us, "I deserve a raise for the hard work I do for *you*." Responding to such signals strengthens employee commitment and loyalty. Those who don't believe they are receiving the increases they deserve or, more specifically, could receive at another organization, are likely to leave. Compensation directors and analysts pay special attention not only to the cost of living, but also to the "cost of labor"—the market rate for attracting and retaining talented employees.

## How Much Is Enough?

The complexities arise when organizations determine "how much." What is the compensation amount that will spur loyalty and productivity? And how does that amount change each year? In other words, how much money will it take to motivate each employee to stay and perform?

Pay can motivate employees to stay by increasing their perceptions of the extent to which their organization supports *them*.[4] It makes sense. Employees think, "If my organization supports me and my welfare, then I'll respond in kind." This leads to higher employee commitment. In our data, we find a strong relationship between employees' ratings of pay and their intent to leave their organizations. In fact, the percentage of employees who rate their pay as poor or very poor and who are considering leaving in the next twelve months was double the rate for those who rate their pay as good or very good (see Figure 6.1).

**Figure 6.1. Impact of Rating of Pay on Intent to Leave**

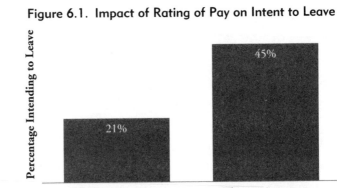

Percentage Intending to Leave

21%

45%

Those rating pay as
good or very good

Those rating pay as
poor or very poor

With regard to motivating employees to perform, academics have traditionally thought of pay as a "hygiene factor"—an element of work that does not motivate, but that, if perceived as unfairly low or inequitable, can de-motivate employees.[5] But surely pay can motivate employees to work harder, right? After all, we work in a climate in which the phrase "pay for performance" is ubiquitous.

Despite conventional wisdom, the research on the subject of pay and performance is not as supportive as we might hope. Some research has shown that pay is related to *quantity* but not *quality* of work.[6] Other research has shown that flexible or incentive-based pay neither motivates nor improves employees' job satisfaction, but that simple fixed pay raises do.[7] The complex relationship among pay, employee motivation, and performance is still being sorted out.

# The Compensation Package

Complexities are exponentially compounded when we consider not only the amount of pay but the push and pull of devising the right compensation package. According to our data, salary is clearly the most important element of the package, but benefits have the potential to become increasingly important. In the United States, employees are expected to pick up an increasingly larger part of the health care tab every year. If that trend continues, then benefits will loom larger in the employees' minds.

The importance of cash-to-benefits varies by country. Of those who stated that compensation is what they want most from an organization, the relative percentage of those who want pay, bonuses, or benefits is shown in Figure 6.2. In Japan, for example, pay is paramount, while in Russia the combined role of the bonuses and benefits is as important as base salary. By country, employees vary widely regarding the extent to which they feel benefits and bonuses are important.

Figure 6.2. The Compensation Components Employees Most Want,
by Country

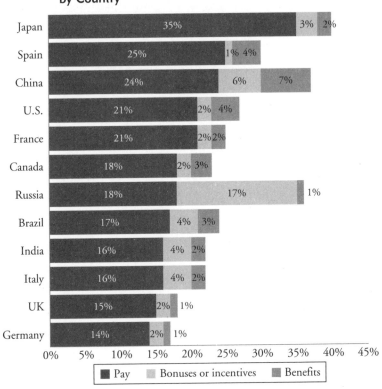

Each country has its own version of "traditional" compensation practices and policies, and we would assume that culture and macroeconomics play a large role. Surprisingly, there is very little empirical research on the impact of these forces on compensation practices. We do know that compensation practices generally follow cultural inclinations. For instance, employees in countries that are risk-averse culturally (or in academic terms high on uncertainty avoidance), such as Germany, China, and the UK, prefer fixed compensation plans such as seniority-and skills-based programs. Not surprisingly, employees in countries that are classified as individualistic, valuing individual rights and freedoms over societal or collective interests, such as Italy and Brazil, prefer individual, rather than team- or group-based incentive programs.[8]

# Is Chen Happy with His Pay?

Is anyone really happy with his or her pay? Do we always want more? Actually, some employees are satisfied with their pay. Thirty-nine percent of employees like Chen Lei, who are the younger male employees in our Confucian Asian countries (China and Japan), rate their pay as good or very good. Internationally, across all types of employees, 42 percent rate their pay as good or very good, while 50 percent think they are paid *fairly*, suggesting that a small segment of employees might not be happy with their pay, but they understand why they are being paid as they are. Even so, the other half of employees are looking for more remuneration. Couple that finding with the fact that 57 percent of employees believe they could find another job that pays them the same or even more. That means more than half of the workforce believes they could jump ship without any impact to their personal finances, and that they could do even better.

What should be more troubling for organizations is that a full third of employees who think they could earn more by leaving are actually considering doing so in the next twelve months. For employees who think finding another well-paying job is unlikely, only 25 percent would consider a move. For a company, that's not a great position to be in, because it suggests that the employees with the most potential are the ones most likely to leave. In other words, Chen is pretty happy with his pay—it's reasonably fair—but if he can make more somewhere else, he'll probably leave.

# Why Money Matters to Employees

Money is the medium with which we provide the basic necessities of life. We work to put food on the table, shelter our families, and clothe our children. Beyond the necessities, we work to buy the things that contribute to the enjoyment we get out of life, regardless of the differences in each person's wants and needs. We come to trust that the check will be in our bank account; we fabricate a standard of living based on it. In many ways, employer and employee are held together by the glue that is compensation. Pay works on two motivational platforms. It provides for necessities and ensures comfort and stability. On another level it allows people to pursue hobbies, pastimes, and just plain *fun*.

For those just trying to feed and clothe themselves, governments around the world have set up minimum wages. Figure 6.3 shows the minimum gross annual wage, pegged against the purchasing power of a dollar in the U.S., otherwise known as the Geary-Khamis or International dollar.[9,10] For the sake of context, the U.S. government defines someone as living in poverty when his or her income is less than $21,954 for a family of four and $10,956 for an individual. In 2009, 14.3 percent of U.S. residents lived in poverty.[11]

### Figure 6.3. Gross Annual Minimum Wage (International Dollars)

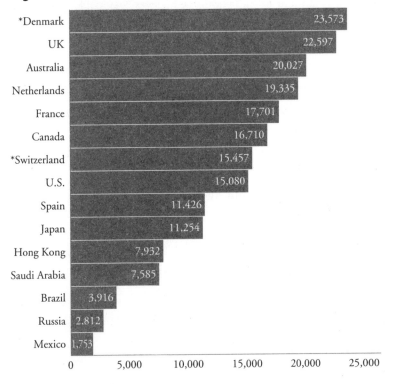

*See Note 11.

If the United States is any indication, the minimum wage falls far short of typical annual expenditures. The most recent data published says that the average household spent $49,638 annually.[12] For some, the motivation to work is rooted in the basic necessities of life; money matters because there are bills to pay.

Money helps people meet physical and emotional needs, but does money spur productivity at work? Does a well-paid employee work harder than a financially challenged counterpart? As we mentioned above, the research on the subject is mixed. According to our own data, we found that, well, it depends. Earlier research demonstrated that for production, warehouse, or clerical workers making less than $40,000 a year, income is positively related to employee engagement—more money equals increased engagement.[13] While the relationship is modest, it is indeed significant. However, as income rises for professional/technical workers and management, the relationship decreases. In other words, income matters more to employee engagement for those making less, but above a certain point there is no relationship.

## Executive Compensation

Executive pay has been in the forefront of the business news since the Enron drama back in 2001. More recently, the public cried foul over bonuses paid to employees at bailed-out firms like Morgan Stanley and Citigroup—a move that contributed to legislation capping their bonuses in the future. During the worst months of the Great Recession, Goldman Sachs also offered bonuses to executives, angering the public and some shareholders. It wasn't just pay in finance that has outraged much of the public. In 2009, public health insurer Blue Cross/Blue Shield's CEO's income rose 26 percent while its net income dropped 49 percent.[14]

It's big money. A ranking of largest executive bonuses of the last decade showed Steve Jobs at Apple in first place making $43 *million* in 2001.[15] Even the losers on this list are big winners. Tied in tenth place, Gary Cohn, president and COO, and Jon Winkleried, retired president and COO of Goldman Sachs, each earned more than $26.7 million in 2006 alone. If you sum up the top ten bonuses, they equal $100 million *more* than the GDP (PPP) of Micronesia.[16]

Vestiges of an economic boom? Not likely. In 2008, the worst economic year since the Great Depression, Wall Street bonuses were the sixth largest on record, with $18.4 billion in bonuses being doled out. That was a decrease of 44 percent since 2007.

Granted, bonuses do not represent the totality of executives' compensation packages, and, taken out of context, it's hard to evaluate their appropriateness. The media focuses on bonuses because the prevailing logic would correlate them with performance. If net income or gross profits rise by "X" percent, bonuses should increase commensurately. Often, no direct relationship is evident.

There is good news and there is bad news when we look at executives' ratings of their own pay. On the positive side, there is, in fact, a relationship between organizational improvement and executive pay. Generally, executives who preside over a growing business report better pay than those in floundering organizations.[17] As performance improves, executives are more likely to rate their pay as good or very good. (See Table 6.1.)

However, the relationship is not as strong when organizational performance is on the decline. When executives rate their organizations' performance as poor, 25 percent continued to rate their pay as very good or good. These data suggest that, when things are good, pay is *really* good, but when performance declines, pay is not as bad as it might be (or, perhaps, should be).

**Table 6.1. Executive Ratings of Pay Under Different Performance Conditions**

| In Past Twelve Months Organizational Performance Has: | Percent of Executives Rating Their Pay As | | |
|---|---|---|---|
| | Poor | Fair | Good |
| Improved | 9% | 23% | 68% |
| Declined | 44% | 31% | 25% |

Across all types of jobs, industries, and countries, compensation is the cornerstone of employment. The good news is that, for organizations that want to improve their compensation systems, there are ways to make the pay-for-work exchange equitable and fair while keeping human capital costs under control.

# Why Fair Compensation Is Good for Business

Except for the privileged few, we all need to be compensated for the work we perform. Pay and benefits are among the most potent tools organizations use to attract, retain, and motivate talented employees. They are also a large expense: compensation typically represents about 50 percent of operating budgets. Given the importance of pay and benefits to both employee and employer, it follows that pay and benefit programs tend to reflect company values and culture.

That's how it should be, according to compensation expert David J. Wudyka, who strongly encourages organizational leaders to "make the best possible use of your firm's compensation dollars." Wudyka is an advocate of fair compensation and believes fair pay involves three forms of equity: across job categories; among people doing the same job; and within the market.[18]

Pay and benefits can mean different things in different countries, but for our purposes pay means fixed salary or wages plus variable bonuses or lump sum merit pay. Benefits represent health insurance, retirement funds, company merchandise discounts, and other perks. Grouped together, the two elements comprise total compensation.

How employees view their total compensation can have an enormous impact on the success of a business or organization. In its most elemental form, compensation helps companies attract qualified applicants and retain valuable employees. But research also shows that high-quality compensation lowers absenteeism and increases everything from employee engagement to productivity and motivation. It can also be an employee catalyst to learn new skills.

The experience of Barclays is relevant to this point. The global financial services provider, which operates in more than fifty countries with more than 144,000 employees, implemented a fair wage program in 2004 by increasing hourly pay rates, providing better benefits, and increasing sick and holiday pay for its London-based cleaning staff. The program resulted in a decline in both absenteeism and turnover—with turnover falling dramatically from 30 to 4 percent. The program also resulted in better customer service and higher customer satisfaction.[19]

# Factors That Influence How Employees View Their Pay and Benefits

A number of factors influence how employees view their pay and benefits, and it is well worth management's time to be familiar with them. Among the most important are:

- *Equity or fairness*. Employees want to be compensated based on what they believe they are worth. They will compare themselves to what they believe others receive, whether inside or outside the organization.
- *Scuttlebutt*. Employees' beliefs about how well they are paid may not match true market information. In the absence of valid information, employees base their pay perceptions on gossip, terminated employees, friends' opinions, recruiters' offers, and plain speculation.
- *Focus on pay, not on benefits*. Benefits are not top-of-mind with most employees, but the more they know about the full features and value of their benefits package, the more satisfied they tend to be.
- *Are managers managing?* If compensation plans are well managed, it can increase the perception that they are fair.
- *Recognition and psychological compensation.* Pay is important, but employees also feel a great sense of reward when co-workers,

customers, senior management, and especially immediate managers respect the value of their work. Career development can also instill a powerful psychological reward. These non-monetary rewards can somewhat compensate for lower pay and benefits.

# Diagnosing Your Organization's Issues with Pay and Benefits

Before taking corrective steps to ensure their employees feel fairly compensated for their contributions, organizations will need to address the following issues and questions:

- Does the organization have a stated compensation policy? Is this communicated to employees? Is the policy aligned with organizational values and goals, as well as with the talent markets?
- To what extent does the organization thoroughly explain the benefits it provides? Does the organization leverage opportunities to promote these offerings with employees?
- What information is available to employees about how well they are paid? Is this information formal or informal? Is this information based in fact or rumor?
- To what extent is pay based on performance? Do employees know what is required of them in order to receive a merit-based pay increase or other variable rewards? Do they feel they have control over the outcomes?
- How much do variable compensation plans actually pay out? Not surprisingly, the more employees receive in direct relationship to their contributions, the more they tend to like the plan.
- To what extent do the pay and benefits programs reflect company values?
- What are the consequences of employee dissatisfaction with their pay or benefits? Will this lead to employee turnover, inability to recruit talented candidates, and poor employee performance?

# Guiding Principles for Fair Compensation

No matter what specific steps an organization takes to support or improve the delivery (or perception) of fair compensation, some essential principles support their effectiveness:

- *Identify what you control*. While budgets may be fixed, managers may have flexibility in distributing rewards. Also, they can identify the pockets of dissatisfaction. Would some clarifications, adjustments, or alternatives help? Managers are responsible for knowing what motivates their employees. Even if they cannot control policies, they can get a better grasp of what employees want and pass that information along to the human resources function.

- *Understand and fairly implement existing programs*. It is important for managers to be up-front in how they communicate salary adjustments. Their job is to manage, as best they can, their organization's policies and budgets. The manager should promote the advantages of the current programs and be frank about their disadvantages.

  It is incumbent upon the manager to know what benefits the organization offers and to look for ways to promote these to employees. Critical also is keeping rewards linked to performance. When raises are based on merit, employees need to know what they did to earn them. Simply saying, "This is all I could give you" is not a demonstration of leadership.

  Consider this creative approach taken by a leadership consulting firm. The You Business LLC, a leadership consulting firm in New York City, not only upgraded the titles of employees, which was a free and easy way to make the employees feel good, but it also let employees choose where they worked (at a home office or at the company's headquarters, for example), and when they worked (9 to 5, early morning, or late at night). To offset the lack of pay raises, the company created a handsome bonus-incentive program that rewards employees for revenue generated from their work. The firm switched from fixed costs to variable costs and continued to make employees feel fairly compensated.[20]

- **Compensate with other recognition and rewards.** Managers should strive to keep employees feeling psychologically rewarded. Aside from formal benefits, there are quite a few other benefits that managers can control, such as department celebrations, new equipment, time off, telecommuting, and flexible hours.

## Concrete Actions to Improve Delivery of Fair Compensation

- **Review compensation package details with your employees.** Provide employees market information about how much the company pays compared to the market. Give them a sense of company-wide compensation. Clarify criteria for salary adjustments. For example, TCP, a world leader in energy-efficient lighting, posts an overview of its compensation strategy on its website. The program focuses on ensuring that pay is competitive within the job market for comparable positions, fair across similar positions within the company, performance-based, and rewards employees and teams for their progress against goals.
- **Create an annual compensation and benefits review.** Create a one-page summary of all company-sponsored pay and benefits. This should include the monetary value of benefits employees might not consider (health insurance, retirement plan contributions, or other subsidized benefits such as tuition assistance). Often these summaries reflect quite a bit more than employees realized. It can generate a sense of employee pride in how much the organization invests in them.
- **Give employees time off.** If policies allow, managers should reward deserving employees with time off. Consider this example: In 2010, during a time when many employers were cutting benefits, the owner of Springboard Public Relations enhanced company benefits in effort to "retain good employees." The eight-person Marlboro, New Jersey, firm changed its maternity-leave policy to include four weeks of paid time off. The owner also extended the offer to include paid paternity leave.[21]

# THE NOVARTIS LIVING WAGE PROGRAM

Novartis Group Companies specializes in improving health and well-being and curing disease. Headquartered in Basel, Switzerland, the company operates in more than 140 countries and employs more than one hundred thousand associates. It's not just the company's mission and size that are impressive. Recently, Novartis became one of the first international companies to voluntarily implement a living wage for its entire workforce.

The process started in 2000 when the Novartis Foundation for Sustainable Development (NFSD) determined that even the lowest salaries paid by Novartis surpassed the basic needs of a worker's family based on local currencies. A second analysis completed by the Indian Research Institute took into account factors such as poverty level, subsistence level, and comfort level and found multiple definitions of a living wage. In other words, a living wage to one family isn't necessarily the same as a living wage for another.

Novartis then teamed up with the Business for Social Responsibility (BSR) to establish a method to calculate living wage levels around the world. Starting with those calculations, Novartis began its living wage program, regularly consulting with local management in countries to ensure pay equity given various economic systems and standards of living.

By 2006, the pay of ninety-three thousand employees had been aligned with living wage levels. Meanwhile, Novartis and BSR have continued to improve by making regular adjustments to the wage calculations and local inflation. It was a team effort from a global company, as Novartis found that local management's active participation was critical to upholding living wages as a "core principle of a company's operations and culture."[22]

- **Explain your benefits package to new hires.** Don't count on new hires reading the employee handbook—they're going to hit the ground running and often don't have time to familiarize themselves with it. Managers should outline company benefits, taking time to emphasize the unique and most valuable features. Organizations work hard to attract and hire prospective employees, and promoting the company's benefits needs to continue after the first day on the job.

- **Find opportunities to remind employees about useful benefits.** Does your company offer tuition assistance? If so, do your employees know that? Do you have employees running late to work a lot? If so, remind them about your organization's mass transit ticket purchase program. In short, if your company offers unique benefits, remind your employees and help them take advantage of them.

Heavy Construction Systems Specialists (HCSS), a Houston-area software developer, takes this concept a step further. It set out to do more than just adequately pay employees; it also assisted them personally and professionally with a solid wellness program. Its headquarters has a jogging trail, putting green, and basketball court, and the company offers yoga, Pilates, and exercise classes on-site.

Employees can receive $100 for good results in their annual health screening (such as healthy cholesterol levels). It doesn't stop at the gym either. Employees collectively own close to 30 percent of the company through a stock-purchase plan, and in 2008 employees received a profit-sharing contribution of cash and stock valued at 22 percent of their salaries.[23]

# 7

# Education and Career Growth

**K**ATIA RETRIEVES her high heels from her bag. Slipping off her fur-lined boots, she curls her toes, willing the blood to return before once again cutting off the supply by putting on her pointy-toed heels. Her hat now removed, she wonders why she bothered combing her hair this morning. "Great start. Barefoot and hair like a haystack," she thinks to herself as she waits for her face to warm up. It's cold—strike that—it's *frigid* in Moscow.

What Katia can't see, she can hear. As the supervisor of analysts at a multinational bank, her intra-office window faces a pit of desks and computer screens. Her door slightly ajar, the din of work invades the quiet of her office. There is a cacophony of computer bells and beeps, louder-than-appropriate speakerphone conversations, coffee mugs hitting desks, the clicking of keyboards, and one annoying squeaky office chair wheel.

She clicks on her space heater and it's down to business. Not as surprised as she should be, she notes the sheer volume in her email inbox—131 new messages since 6:00 p.m. yesterday. Many of them are the usual; she scans through industry blasts, administrative what-nots, SUPER CRITICAL meeting invitations, all of which she ignores. (As a rule, she finds that anyone who needs to use ALL CAPS never truly has anything important to say or the caps would be superfluous. Plus, there's slight disdain generated from being e-yelled-at that she usually fails to overcome.)

An email from HR catches her eye. Subject: "Management Training." Katia takes a sip of coffee and clicks. Since accepting this job two years ago, Katia has kept an eye out for career opportunities. She's been warned that it's a competitive process and that those being considered aren't afraid to throw a punch or two. Judging from the number of skirts in upper management positions, she guesses that it's more difficult for a woman.

Reading further, the process seems straightforward enough: tell your manager you are interested, pull together a statement of intent to explain why you are a good choice for the program, and send in your résumé. Katia looks for the catch and quickly finds it. "Candidates will be expected to continue their normal daily duties, but should plan on logging an additional fifteen hours a week during the program."

She mulls it over. If she signs up, so much for seeing her friends and boyfriend this spring: HR's policy is tantamount to a sixty-five-hour workweek. Then again, she's going to need some kind of boost if she ever wants to jump past middle management. Her résumé is a mess, but her boss has confidence in her and she's sure he'd sponsor her candidacy. Compared with going back to school for a management degree, this seems like the easier path.

"No time like the present," Katia resolves and sends the application email to her boss. She's committed herself to the next step in her career.

# In Pursuit of Learning and Advancement

For Katia, there is a choice to be made: education and career advancement or personal time. Maybe we've all faced that choice at one point or another. Some of us have made a choice to invest countless hours and years on fancy degrees. Others sign up for grueling management training programs that have schedules more like a medical residency program than a desk job. Still others pick à la carte training, accept challenging assignments, or transfer their skills into a new industry.

Employees who responded to our survey that education and career growth were what they wanted most from their company are on a mission to improve themselves and their stations, seeking fair promotion opportunities and accessible development options. These employees stated what they most wanted from their employer was

- "A chance to improve and advance"
- "Good leadership that is interested in my personal and professional development"
- "Clear development path"
- "Professional development"
- "Fair career opportunities"
- "Career prospects"
- "I want to see the potential for a growth opportunity"
- "Reduce nepotism and only promote workers using the merit principle"
- "To move into management"

*Carpe diem*! Many employees seize on their company's educational opportunities or brave uncharted territory and make opportunities for themselves. In the United States, the number of students earning their bachelor's and master's degrees has risen dramatically since 1960. In the past fifty years the number of bachelor's degrees conferred annually has grown from under four hundred thousand to 1.5 million, and there are over eight times more master's degrees conferred.[1]

Employees want education, training, and career development. As we'll see, helping them attain it is a win for business and a win for employees. Beyond the business economics, humans have an innate drive to learn and grow. We all have felt it: the need to improve, to develop a new skill, to take the next step, to master the next challenge. The most highly regarded, time-tested and universally accepted theories have described the phenomenon as self-perfecting drive[2,3] or self-actualization.[4,5]

Personal economics also play a role in an individual's motivation to advance. Some people feel the need to continually grow their financial portfolios and perhaps commensurately accrue symbols of wealth. For all of us, let's face it: the cost of living continues to climb. Career advancement might be a means to an end—a higher salary to fit a higher cost of living.

Six percent of employees cited career development as the *most* important thing they wanted from the employer, and an additional 3 percent reported they wanted training or development. Almost one of every ten employees is pining for education or career growth.

# Is Katia Receiving the Development She Needs?

For younger generation (Millennial or Generation X) Russian employees in the financial sector like Katia, opportunity for learning exists—67 percent report that they are given a "real opportunity" to improve their skills in their company. The worldwide average stands at only 57 percent.

But the question becomes: Can these new skills be used on the job? While some learning will obviously be used in an employee's current job, much of new skill development is in pursuit of the next career step. This distinction between opportunity for skill improvement and opportunity for career development is an important one and highlights the issue: while many employees feel they can do their jobs well—and have the tools to do so—they don't have much hope of advancing. While globally the number of employees who have opportunities to learn (57 percent) roughly matches those who feel they can meet their career goals with their current employer (52 percent), the situation for employees like Katia is more bleak. For Katia and her counterparts, 67 percent believe their current employer provides the opportunity for skill improvement, but only 47 percent feel they will be able to achieve their career goals with their current employers. Clearly, some development investment appears wasted on those with no chance of advancing.

For businesses, the lesson is to identify human capital needs in conjunction with identifying those likely to make career strides ("high-potentials") and invest early and often in their development. If businesses don't support career development, what they're really doing is encouraging their employees to leave once they've mastered their existing skills. If employees aren't able to envision their futures within their current organization, they'll simply look over the fence. A stunning 54 percent of employees who can't see a path to advancement are considering leaving.

It can work on the positive side, too. If employees believe they can achieve their career goals within their companies, only 19 percent are seriously considering leaving their organizations in the next twelve months (see Figure 7.1). In other words, the risk of losing valuable employees drops by more than half simply by providing career development.

**Figure 7.1. Impact of Career Opportunities on Intent to Leave**

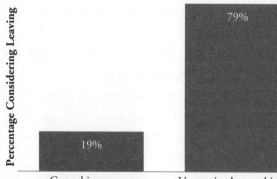

This risk translates into real money that might be spent recovering from turnover. Although experts disagree on the formula for calculating the cost of turnover,[6] and such formulas yield widely varying estimates depending on job and industry,[7] for the sake of argument, let's accept a conservative U.S.-based estimate: 25 percent of an employee's annual salary.[8] That's $13,355 on average per employee.

Apply that number to an entire organization and we quickly see that turnover is an expensive proposition. Let's say you employ 7,500 employees. According to our data, 48 percent of employees are not confident they can achieve their career goals at their current employer. Seventy-nine percent of that group will consider leaving that same year. Let's assume only half of them do. Given those statistics and the average cost of turnover, your company faces turnover costs of $79,128,375. Most companies simply can't afford to ignore the gap between what employees want and what they are receiving in terms of development and advancement opportunities.

# Why Career Education and Growth Matter to Your Employees

When employees have the knowledge, skills, and tools to do their jobs effectively, they are clearly going to be more productive and engaged. Beyond skills training, employee can have a wide variety of long-term career development objectives. Employees want to believe they are achieving or making progress toward their objectives. They want to believe that their current jobs, in their current organizations, are an important part of achieving those objectives.

Meeting employee needs for education and growth means preparing them for the demands of their current jobs and supporting them in their longer-term career objectives. Most organizations view it as their responsibility to create a supportive environment for learning job skills and experiencing professional growth, yet many companies see their employees as primarily responsible for creating their own opportunities.

Employees want to feel they know how to perform their current assignments. New employees expect and want orientation, education, and training to achieve proficiency in their tasks. In addition, when organizational change occurs, special training is often required so that employees can successfully deliver against the new demands of their jobs. Research has proven that such training systems are integral to organizational success.

Additionally, a sense of making progress toward personal career objectives is a key driver of employee retention.[9] Career development no longer means strictly vertical promotions, but includes the sequence of job changes that employees make during their working lives.

---

*Education and growth are more important when:*

- Employee turnover is high
- Expectations or job demands change frequently
- Labor market conditions make it difficult to hire workers with needed skills
- Employees are working within a unique or complex business

*Education and growth are less important when:*

- Employee skill sets are stable and don't need to change
- Turnover is low
- The organization is able to select new employees with the required skills and knowledge

---

# Why Career Education and Growth Are Good for Business—Now and into the Future

It goes without saying that organizations need well-trained workers; goals cannot be achieved without them. Intuitively, this makes sense to any manager, but it also should make sense to CEOs, chief financial officers, and anybody else with responsibility for managing a profit-and-loss statement. Companies that invest in training and development reap the rewards in terms of higher net sales and increased gross profits.

Dr. Laurie Bassi, an economist and HR specialist, identified this trend more than a decade ago while working at the American Society for Training and Development. Bassi set out to compare the market-to-book ratio of companies that spent more than average on training and development against those that spent less than average.[10] Market-to-book compares the market value of a company's outstanding shares against the firm's "book" value—its net assets minus liabilities. It's a tool used by sophisticated investors to determine whether companies are creating value. The higher the market-to-book ratio, the more value that's created. Bassi's original research analyzed companies' financial performance during 1996 and 1997, and she found that organizations that were above the median in per-employee training expenditures increased their market-to-book ratio on average by more than double compared to spenders below the median.

So Bassi and her business partner Dan McMurrer started an investment fund, Bassi Investments, that focused on companies that spend more in training than their business counterparts. The fund outperformed the S&P.

Beyond the financial motivations for creating a high-performing workforce, another impetus for employee development looms. Across North America, Europe, and parts of Asia, the Baby Boomer phenomenon is projected to leave a skill gap that portends a talent chasm in the managerial ranks. As posts are abandoned by their Boomer sentries, will organizations and employees stumble in the absence of leadership? Leaders must educate workers for the future, to be sure, but also ready them for promotion—and in short order.

The sun has started to set on the day of the Baby Boomer[11]; in the late 1980s, they accounted for 61 percent of the workforce. Their numbers have since dwindled to 45 percent and will slowly decline until 2025 (see Figure 7.2). It's important to remember that the Millennial generation is large in its own right at more than eighty-three million strong (in fact, currently five million larger than the Boomer generation), and they tend to have very positive attitudes about work and their ability to excel.[12] We found that Millennials tout their own training and are more optimistic about their career advancement opportunities than either the Boomers or Gen-Xers (see Figure 7.3). However, while younger employees bring unique talents and a fresh perspective, it's equally true that they lack the deep expertise gained through extended work

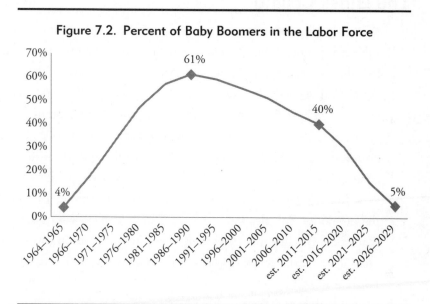

Figure 7.2.  Percent of Baby Boomers in the Labor Force

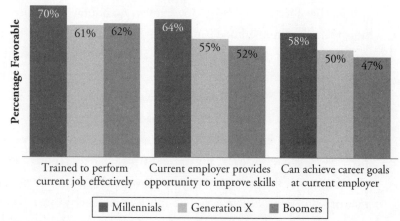

Figure 7.3.  Views of Career Opportunities by Global
Generational Groups

experiences and accumulated training. Not only does today's performance depend on a skilled workforce, but so does future performance. That's why we believe strongly that organizations must invest in workforce education *right now*.

# The Glass Ceiling

We can hardly comment on career goals and paths without broaching the subject of the glass ceiling, a ubiquitous phrase that refers to the seemingly invisible barrier keeping women out of the executive ranks. In the United States, findings from the Government Accountability Office and reported by *The New York Times* and *The Wall Street Journal* demonstrate that the ceiling remains intact. Today, women hold just 40 percent of managerial positions and make $0.81 on the dollar when compared to their male counterparts,[13] and the number of female executives declines as rank rises. In 2007 The White House Project, a bipartisan group dedicated to the promotion and election of women into leadership positions, found that women occupy just 16 percent of executive leadership suites—and only 15 percent occupy a board seat. In 2008, a mere 3 percent of Fortune 500 CEOs were women.[14]

Internationally, the trend holds. As employees move up the ranks, the ratio of women to men becomes increasingly imbalanced (see Figure 7.4).

The big question is *why?* A Government Accountability Office report noted that the "motherhood penalty" might play a role. Mother-to-father pay ratio was less than even that of women-to-men: $0.79 on the dollar. Sixty-three percent of women managers were childless, compared to 57 percent of men. While 59 percent of women managers were married, this compared to 74 percent for male managers.

Interestingly, employees tell us that their male and female managers perform equally effectively, for the most part. Direct reports rated the performance of the managers near equally, whether their managers were men or women (see Figure 7.5). The only level at which women managers don't essentially have parity with male counterparts is at the mid-manager level. Here, women managers' performance lags behind men's by four percentage points. This small difference is worth more investigation, but given the equality of performance on the rest of the leadership ladder, there may be something unique about this career rung. If true, the data suggests that women may need additional training opportunities or job support at the mid-manager level.

**Figure 7.4.** **Proportion of Men and Women in Management Positions**

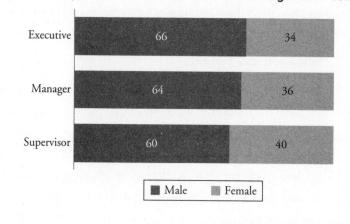

**Figure 7.5.** Views of Career Opportunities by Men and Women at Different Managerial Levels

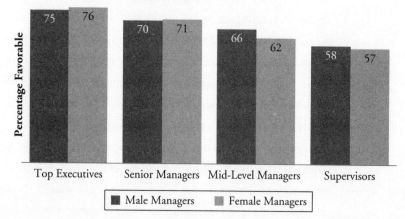

# Influencing Employee Education and Growth the Right Way

While the topic "education and growth" represents one of seven things employees most want, in reality this broader topic can be separated into two distinct but interrelated sub-topics. Education is akin to training and more focused on job skills. On the other hand, growth is fundamentally focused on long-term career development. We outline the factors that influence employee perceptions of both as well as broader organizational factors that affect how employees view the organizational support for education and growth.

### Education and Training

- *Formal support for education and training.* Organizations differ significantly when it comes to the depth and quality of education and training provided. Some examples of strong organizational support include emphasizing the importance of new-employee training, providing budget and time for training, and having supervisors who are attentive to the training needs of their employees and who reward and support employees when they demonstrate new skills and knowledge.

  In 2004, in the midst of global expansion, Wal-Mart focused on talent development efforts intended to build competencies among business-technology leaders. One initiative included a leader-in-training program developed to prepare those closest to the work to take on more responsibility. Another effort was implemented to track employees' goals and skills so the company could recommend appropriate training and work experiences. Wal-Mart viewed these talent development efforts as both a survival tactic and as a competitive advantage.[15]

- *Design and implementation.* Training and education programs must fit the needs and interests of employees as well as the organization. For example, when the level of training (beginner, intermediate, advanced) is appropriate, employees naturally view the training and education as more useful and are more motivated to participate. Of course, how programs are implemented—including the techniques used and skill and enthusiasm level of trainers—significantly impacts effectiveness.

- *Cross-training.* Not only does cross-training allow a business to adapt during employee vacations or sick time, but it gives employees a sense of security and versatility. Cross-training also allows managers to redeploy employees away from traditional assignments, allowing others to step into the gap. A lack of cross-training (or bad cross-training) can be a serious contributor to dissatisfaction, as employees feel ill-equipped to perform new tasks, and work is left undone.

## Growth and Development Planning

- *Expectations for career milestones.* Managers should communicate realistic expectations for career opportunities by laying out career paths for employees and highlighting the experience required for promotions. Without this information, employees will have their own expectations based on their observations and self-assessments of their own capabilities. These self-assessments can be overly optimistic or overly pessimistic, and either can have a negative impact on performance.

- *Explicit growth and development discussions.* Using annual performance feedback as a foundation, managers should initiate ongoing career and planning discussions with their direct reports.

---

**Top Barriers to Development**

What employees typically say:

- Leaders don't support development
  - Management only pays lip service to employee development
  - There is no money in the budget
  - HR tries, but they just aren't supported at the top

> • Development won't make a difference
> • Promotions still depend on who you know
> • This is another fad-of-the-month
> • I don't have enough time
> • Just doing my job takes more time than I have
> • I am rewarded for results, not personal development
> • It is not a priority in light of everything else I have to do

# How to Diagnose Your Organization's Education and Growth Issue

Before managers can determine "how" to fix an education and growth deficiency, they must understand what the problem is and why it exists. Below are some fundamental issues or questions for managers and their teams to consider.

### Diagnosing Education and Training Issues

- What is causing the gap between employee performance and capabilities? Is it due to changing work processes, standards or expectations, new technologies, shifting markets, or customer requirements?
- Who needs to be trained and why? Under what circumstances do employees feel unprepared?
- What kind of new-employee training is available? How quickly do employees gain proficiency?
- Beyond formal training, could other education and training solutions help? For example, what role could coaching, mentoring, job-performance aids, help systems, cross-training, and reference guides play?
- After formal education and training programs, is there other support for employees? Do supervisors provide resources (such as

time) to reinforce confidence and new learning? Do peers support one another? Do employees feel recognized and rewarded for demonstrating new skills?

---

### Characteristics of Effective Training

- Training is related to clear business and development needs.
- Objectives are clearly specified and understood by participants.
- Program design incorporates principles of adult learning (for example, adults learn when they need to and have different learning styles).
- Support, in the form of appropriate resources and supervisory/peer encouragement for using new skills, is apparent.
- Training content is appropriately matched to skill and knowledge levels of participants.

---

## Diagnosing Employee Growth and Development Issues

- In general, how well do managers understand the growth and development objectives of their employees? What stands in the way of employees achieving those objectives?
- What information do employees use to envision their future careers with the organization? To what extent do they rely on tracking promotions, formal career paths, or company gossip?
- How do your best employees view their future with the organization? Would they characterize favorably their career-related conversations to date?
- How does the organization provide new employees with growth and development expectations?
- How does the organization keep its "B" players interested in continuing to grow, develop, and contribute to the organization?

# Guiding Principles to Ensure Education and Growth Opportunities

No matter what specific steps an organization may take to enhance the employee experience of education and growth, some essential principles underlie any effective action. They include:

- *Identify development needs.* Enhancing employee skills and abilities through education and training is not always the answer for improving job performance. Other factors, such as clear performance expectations, appropriate resources, supervisory support, and performance feedback, also influence employee performance. Education and training are critical when changes in individual knowledge, skills, or abilities affect performance on the job.

  Anticipating growth and the need to meet new standards for certification is what caused Bright Horizons Family Solutions, a national day care provider based in Watertown, Massachusetts, to institute a new program for its teachers. The online child development associate program helped provide its teachers with the knowledge required to meet industry certification requirements.[16] Over the past ten years, Kimberly-Clark, a multinational maker of paper and personal care products, has worked to improve talent development for its rapidly growing overseas markets. Since the initiative began, average training time for Latin America–based employees has skyrocketed to thirty-eight hours per year. Much of the training has focused on dramatically improving the manufacturing skills of the blue-collar workforce. The company has also implemented a program to build social and interpersonal skills. On a lighter note, the company also promotes the pursuit of non-work skills to employees by providing things like piano lessons.[17]

- *Provide support.* If employees perceive or experience barriers to using newly acquired knowledge or skills, then the value of these programs drops considerably. When such barriers exist, employees naturally approach training or other programs with greater skepticism. Typical barriers include lack of recognition, a dearth of supervisory or peer support, and little expectation of actually using newly acquired knowledge.

When job demands frequently change, organizations need to provide continuous learning opportunities and devise formal reward systems that reinforce and promote training opportunities. Among other programs intended to improve work/life balance and provide career development for sailors, the U.S. Navy offers tuition assistance for associate's and bachelor's degrees as well as other educational opportunities.[18]

Gensler, a global architecture, design, planning, and strategic consulting firm, implemented a Talent Development Studio to centralize, structure, and refocus its talent development efforts. The studio helped the firm stay competitive and helped employees keep up with changing certification and accreditation needs. By using live classes as well as webcasts, the studio has been able to provide education and development programs to multiple offices on topics such as "green design" and electronic design software.[19]

- *Promote organizational success.* It is incumbent upon managers to understand the resources the company has to offer. For example, a manager can find mentors or role models for employees. Mentoring programs are generally viewed by employees as an excellent means of personal and career development. A skilled manager will also work with employees to envision what a promising future with the organization looks like. Managers should always link growth and development to organizational success, emphasizing that the best opportunities go to those who contribute the most.

Sometimes an organization has to go outside to achieve success with its training and development efforts. With 35 percent of its workforce becoming eligible for retirement within the next five years and low retention rates at its South Florida nuclear plant, leaders at Florida Power & Light began looking for ways to hire, develop, and retain talent. To do so, Florida Power & Light offered training and development through the local community college—Miami Dade College—which had strong ties with the largely Hispanic community.[20]

# Actions to Improve the Employee Experience of Education and Growth

For leaders, meeting employees' needs for growth and development should be a no-brainer. Like processing raw materials, organizations have an opportunity to *create* value. With minimal investment, employees can transform themselves into a more valuable resource, fulfilling both their own needs for development as well as their organization's need for a renewable, high-performing workforce. The actions that an organization and its managers undertake to promote education and growth must address well-understood specific needs. The following are ideas offered to help you start:

- *Develop a thorough employee orientation process.* Orientation programs provide an excellent opportunity to communicate information about the company and its mission, vision, and values. Some organizations employ a "buddy system," with veteran employees pairing up with new employees to answer questions about performance expectations and policies and to provide general information about the company.
- *Create individual education and growth plans for employees.* Define areas in which employees should enhance their abilities. This creates a context for education or other skill development.
- *Conduct systematic evaluations of the organization's education and training programs.* As a general rule, organizations should determine whether their training programs are adding value. It's difficult to quantify the financial impact of a training program, but

it is relatively easy to survey employees and determine whether they valued the training, gained knowledge, and are using the skills they learned.

- *Promote the organization's job posting system.* Even if there are no good matches for employees, it still gives them confidence that they will know when the right job comes along.
- *Hold luncheon workshops or "brown bag" sessions.* These can be used to keep employees current on industry, business, and career trends. Bringing in guest speakers to tell stories of their own development is a popular option.
- *Use education and training as preparation for career moves.* For example, an organization might still send a high-potential employee to manager training, even if a position is not open. The employee will respect the gesture as an investment in his or her career.

---

**Career Development Without Promotions**

- Career growth and development is not just about vertical promotions. That may not be what organizations can offer or what employees always want. Consider the following options to help employees move toward their career objectives:
  - Assignment to large-scale, visible projects
  - Access to the latest technology
  - Job rotation—trading duties with someone else
  - Flexible hours or part-time opportunities
  - Training on a future-oriented skill
  - Project leadership
  - Participation in high-level meetings
  - Lateral transfers—moving sideways in the organization, not necessarily up
  - Provide status perks—new job title, public recognition for good work, awards

# 8

# Conditions at Work

**M**IGUEL BRINGS his pickup to a stop in the parking lot of his *maquiladora*. Pausing to note respectfully the ominous gurgle in his stomach, Miguel reaffirms that the third tamale he grabbed at lunch was worth it.

The lunch was a union-sponsored affair at the hall; the draw of free food brought most of the workers from the A shift. Union leaders have been reflecting a general unrest among the workers. If the union's reports about sister-sites in Thailand and Malaysia are true, their factory floors are dark, hot, and overwhelmingly noisy by comparison.

"Conditions could be better," Miguel thinks to himself. "But is this the issue to risk a strike over? Would it do any good?" With unemployment so high, he worries about losing his job. "At least I'm making a decent wage," he argues with himself as he walks into the C gate.

*Meanwhile...*

In the Silicon Valley city of San Jose, Susan unpacks her cafeteria-bought Bento box with tuna and California rolls lying on a wilted piece of lettuce. She sits down in her office chair and lifts the plastic lid to release a whiff of sea and surf. She rips the foil packet of soy sauce with her teeth and unsheathes the chopsticks.

The eight rolls with their quiet, peaceful orderliness appeal to Susan—a calm contrast to her days as HR director managing the movement and issues of employees throughout the international high-tech company. Pre-sushi run, the latest news about the union meeting came from the Chihuahua site. The union has a point, she agrees, but she's just not sure what a show of force is going to do at this point. Budgets have been frozen and "lean" is an understatement when Susan looks at next year's numbers. There are no egregious safety violations, but obviously, the conditions are not comfortable and could be vastly improved. "I wouldn't work there," she admits to herself.

She wields her chopsticks like a samurai and deftly deposits the entire roll in her mouth, hoping no unannounced visitors see her looking like a bulgy-eyed squirrel. She chews furiously and swallows hard.

Not that she usually has too many visitors. It's lonely at the top, especially for a woman in high-tech manufacturing. She doesn't feel she can really talk to her direct reports about everything because it might affect her position of authority. Folks in corporate are nice enough, but being in HR means she has to be tight-lipped about many aspects of her job. It's not like she can comment on rumors of layoffs or laugh about the guy who took his pants off in the lobby two years ago (still an unsolved mystery: Was it because they were too hot or too tight?). Not being a conversationalist by nature only makes the situation worse.

Her team is a tightly knit group, but as its "coach" she stays a bit removed from the others. "That's a good thing," she declares, partly to make herself feel better. At least they have a sense of camaraderie and cooperation; they want to help each other out.

# The Condition of "Conditions"

Miguel and Susan work in very different environments, but they both want decent working conditions. When we began the research for this book, we anticipated that positive physical working conditions, whether in a mine shaft, on an assembly line, or in an office chair, would be among the things that employees wanted. However, we were surprised at how powerful the desire was for a supportive social environment. In fact, of the employees who stated that positive working conditions were the most important thing they wanted from their employer, only 18 percent pointed to physical conditions. The vast majority of them—82 percent—identified positive social conditions.

Employees who mentioned the physical aspects of the job mentioned safety and health concerns, as well as equipment and resource needs. Comments included:

- "Healthy and safe work environment"
- "Safety—to get home each night"
- "I want a work space that is clean, quiet, responsible, and safe"
- "Access to all the tools we are supposed to have available to do our jobs"
- "To offer equipment that is in good working condition, and safe to operate"

Social support means having fun and feeling less stressed. It means having a strong team and being trusted to get the job done. A strong team can be weakened by perceptions of favoritism or inequality; employees told us that they wanted to be treated fairly. Employees who want a socially supportive workplace want to offer opinions and input and, more importantly, to be *heard*, especially by their managers. Along these lines, employees made comments like:

- "There is a need for a healthy, stress-free, and encouraging environment"
- "The workload should be given out more evenly and the daily hours reduced"

- "Understanding that there is a balance between work and home life, that I can't drop everything for work"
- "Fun working environment"
- "I want there to be a feeling of working together as a team"
- "To work in an environment that is free of any type of discrimination"
- "To be taken seriously when I go forward with a concern"
- "Support from management and co-workers when I need someone to back me up, help with the huge volume of workload"
- "Employers should be supporting, helping, caring, and above all, trustworthy and very good human beings!"

Positive working conditions are critically important. Work can stress us out or make us feel at peace. It is dangerous or safe. We feel welcome or ostracized. Regardless of whether it's the social or physical environment, employees want to be comfortable in their surroundings.

# Are Miguel and Susan Comfortable and Safe in Their Workplace Surroundings?

Fifty-nine percent of employees like Miguel—young male production workers in Latin American countries like Mexico and Brazil—rate both their physical work environment and the safety of their workplace as good or very good.[1] Sixty-seven percent say that they have the equipment and tools to do their jobs. When compared to the global averages, employees like Miguel rate their physical work environment higher (53 percent vs. 59 percent, respectively), but their safety lower (65 percent vs. 59 percent). Perhaps for workers like Miguel, these numbers suggest that those who rate their overall physical working conditions more favorably, but their safety lower, accept an element of danger as a condition of their employment.

About half of employees Susan represents—women who are in management in the manufacturing sector—feel supported socially at work. For this type of worker, social conditions tend to trump physical ones. Forty-nine percent of employees like Susan report that stress is reasonable, and 56 percent report that their company supports work/life balance; both elements of work are reported in numbers similar to the global averages (53 percent and 55 percent, respectively).

Are managers like Susan brainstorming, solving problems together, and working as a team? Managers report that they are invited to participate in decisions that affect their work (50 percent). However, more managers like Susan feel a sense of camaraderie; 71 percent of this group feels like part of a team, and that's higher than the international average at 67 percent. But still, almost 30 percent feel like Susan does above—it's lonely at the top.

# Are Workplace Conditions Improving?

With all of the media attention on global workplace conditions, we would expect that organizational leaders are focused on making improvements. And they are. Looking across the longest trend lines available to us, those from the United States, most aspects of work conditions are holding steady or improving.

Since 1990, fewer American employees report poor physical working conditions, although production employees experience conditions that are clearly less favorable than the average employee in the United States experiences (see Figure 8.1).

Social conditions at work affect all types of employees. Looking back to 1995,[2] U.S. employees report that leadership teams have increasingly expressed and demonstrated concern for their well-being, although leaders' caring seems to have dipped slightly during the recent recession. It comes as no surprise that those employees in management positions report higher levels of caring from management than do other types or workers. We might surmise that either they have a clearer line of sight into the considerations of management or, if you are a conspiracy theorist, managers take care of themselves first and foremost. Production employees again lag behind. Even at their peak in 2009, only 45 percent of production workers believed that management was concerned about them (see Figure 8.2).

**Figure 8.1. Ratings of Physical Working Conditions in the United States, 1990–2010**

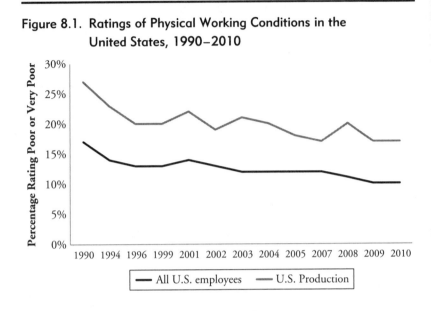

**Figure 8.2. Management Concern for Employee Well-Being in the United States by Selected Job Type, 1995–2010[3]**

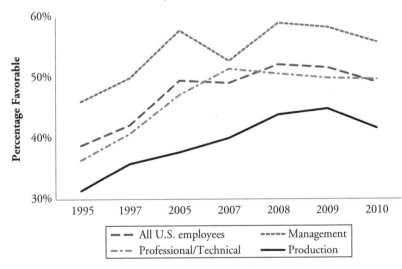

Organizational support for work/life balance has also been on the rise in the United States, but production employees lag behind on this indicator as well (see Figure 8.3). In the world of first, second, and third shifts and production floors, organizations have less opportunity to be flexible. Even so, the trend in year-over-year improvement in the United States remains across the board.

---

**Figure 8.3. Organizational Support for Work/Life Balance in the United States by Selected Job Type, 1993–2010**

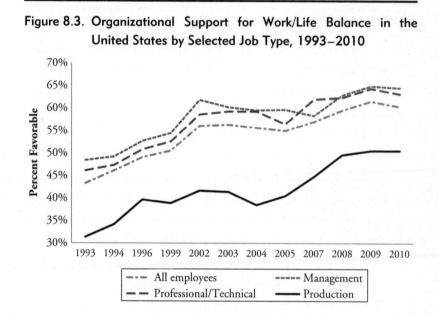

---

# Where Workers Feel Safe and Productive

Over the years, there have been reports of working conditions in various countries that were shocking to those of us who report to a clean, safe office every day. These reports describe, for example, the conditions of sweatshop workers in China, gold mine workers in Africa, and wartime military defense contractors in the Middle East. In 2010, through the safety of our computer screens and televisions, we waited while thirty-three trapped Chilean miners were pulled to safety after being buried alive for a month. Explosions occur in factories seemingly daily: a quick Google search found them in New Hampshire, West Virginia, and

Las Vegas, as well as in China, the UK, and Italy. Egregious working conditions seem to exist everywhere.

Media reports have, at times, been catalysts for action. At the international level, there have been valiant efforts to improve the worst conditions through political pressure. But one tragic incident does not a complete picture make.

In Figure 8.4 we ranked employees' average ratings of their physical and social working conditions. The physical conditions index measured employees' overall ratings of their physical environment, whether employees felt physically safe at work and had the proper equipment to do their jobs. The social conditions index averages favorable responses regarding work stress, work/life balance, feeling of "team," and management's concern for employee well-being.

One trend is clear. Physical working conditions are rated more favorably than social conditions for all but two countries. This may be due to political pressures or mandated national standards. Looking down the ranking, we could have predicted that France would have been in the bottom, given recent news accounts of worker unrest on a national scale.[4] The top two countries, India and China, have both high physical and social working conditions scores; in other words, their social working conditions scores aren't dragging down their average. Workers' social support in these countries helps to improve their overall environment.

China? India? These are not exactly two countries that spring to mind when Western readers think of safe working environments. There could be several reasons for their high scores, including the possibility that, well, things are pretty good there. In China, the country's Confucian and communist roots may play a role. While Confucian principals support a focus on humanity and filial piety, it's also true that underpinning communism is the belief that people should make decisions for the benefit of the group. This focus on the society—the country as a collective, as one—would likely support a value for safe working conditions, encapsulated in a more general value of communal health and well-being.

### Figure 8.4. Country Ranking on Physical and Social Working Conditions

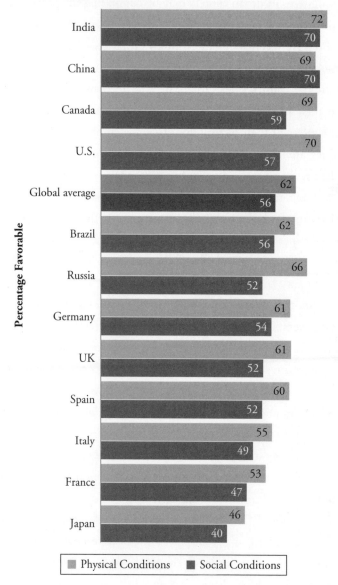

Employees in China, as well as in India, may be making different kinds of comparisons than employees in other countries are making. In India, employees in urban centers may be comparing the peace and cleanliness of their office to the hot, noisy, crowded streets outside. In China, those who have recently migrated to an urban center may be comparing the modernity of the office to their lives of few modern conveniences in the Chinese countryside. Others may be recognizing improvements made to their physical work environment; they aren't necessarily comparing the safety of their factory floor to an assembly line in the United States. They are likely comparing their working conditions to what it was like the previous year—or even five years ago—and undoubtedly there have been big improvements in many of China's and India's factories in that time. The massive economic growth that both China and India have experienced may have ushered in the opportunity, and perhaps expectation, for improvement on this front. Those improvements could be, in part, behind China's and India's high scores.

Another factor that may tip the scale is how and from whom data were collected. Because the WorkTrends survey fuels research on organizational functioning, we collected data from employees in organizations with more than one hundred people. This requirement would exclude some employees, such as those working in smaller, local businesses and family farms. Employees in larger organizations are also more likely to have Internet access, a necessary component for taking the WorkTrends survey, which is administered online.

We surveyed people from every major industry and every job type, and, except for workers in agriculture, our sample approximates the working population in China and India.[5,6,7,8] However, it's also true that the nature of the survey makes it difficult to reach workers in remote areas and excludes those in local, smaller businesses. Would those employees give similarly high ratings to their workplace conditions? Maybe so, but perhaps not.

In general, employees' ratings of their social working conditions lag behind their ratings of their physical working conditions. We might be surprised by this, but the social aspects of one's job are cheaper to attend to than safety issues and the physical environment. On the other hand, social conditions at work are harder to identify and often more difficult to remedy. They rely on employees' feelings of trust and being part of a team, and, once damaged, camaraderie and cooperation are often difficult to repair. When we look across countries, we see that more than double the number of employees rate themselves as "part of a team" if the people working around them are pitching in, if their senior leaders show concern about them, if their managers keep commitments, or if their team members cooperate (see Figure 8.5).

**Figure 8.5.  Impact of Trust and Cooperation on Feeling
           Part of a Team**

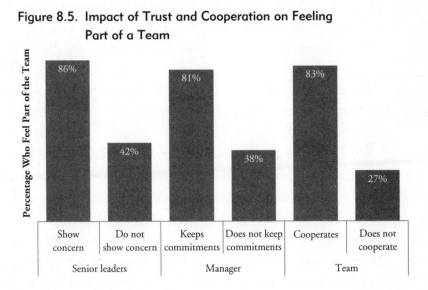

This discussion dispels the stereotype that "working conditions" are the lighting in your office, the percentage of particulates in the air, and the height of your computer monitor. In fact, employees gripe most about the social aspects of work. Strides have been made in improving our physical environs, but now leaders also need to boost their humanity quotient and tune into their employees' needs by offering them support, a strong team, and less stress.

# The Right Way to Influence How Employees View Their Workplace Conditions

Providing employees with positive working conditions boils down to two things: physical working conditions that emphasize health and safety and social working conditions that emphasize teamwork and cooperation and freedom from undue mental and emotional stress. While these two sets of conditions may be interrelated, it's important to address them separately.

# Physical Working Conditions

As noted earlier in this chapter, positive physical working conditions are an important health and productivity concern. This is true of office environments, service settings, and manufacturing plants. What employees want from their physical work environment reflects a concern about their physical safety, but it also has to do with issues such as ventilation, noise, lighting, temperature, hazardous materials, and cleanliness.

A number of management practices can influence how employees experience their physical working conditions. Most obvious among these is the actual physical environment. Different employees have different expectations and standards for what they consider acceptable. A recent accident will certainly make employees more sensitive to safety concerns. Manufacturing employees will be more concerned with machinery, whereas office workers are more likely to be concerned with computer- and technology-related issues. Transportation employees such as truck drivers will be more concerned about highway accidents. Psychological issues come into play as well. For example, in a retail environment, safety concerns might come from cramped and hazardous stockrooms or they might focus on walking alone across a dark parking lot after work.

Before an organization can effectively address potential problems or opportunities, it must have a good understanding of the specific factors that concern employees. Some questions to consider include:

- Beyond regulatory compliance, what are the safety concerns of employees? Are they more important to certain shifts or certain types of employees or during seasonal cycles? When does the concern turn into a "big deal" to employees?
- How does the physical environment dampen productivity, comfort, and health? Are all employees impacted the same, or are there pockets of heightened sensitivity?
- What is the source of concern? Physically, is the concern based on machinery and equipment or on issues such as physical layout, noise, air quality, or temperature? To what extent is the concern related to employee training, experience, or expectations?
- Organizationally, are safety policies effectively communicated and are processes monitored? To what extent do recognition and reward practices support the organization's stated values?
- What practices are in place to gather employee input on working conditions? How are complaints, suggestions, and problems tracked?
- What are the estimated costs of problems? Does this estimate consider employee well-being, public image, and productivity as well as financial costs?

## Guiding Principles to Improve Physical Workplace Conditions

Giving employees what they really need when it comes to physical workplace conditions can be placed into three categories: environment, employee, and organization.

- *Environment.* This includes the traditional "brick and mortar" physical work environment as well as working conditions for remote, telecommuting, or traveling employees. Considerations include equipment design, availability of tools and resources, physical structure and workspaces, air quality, and characteristics of the work location (parking lots, crime rates, etc.).

- *Employee.* Employee considerations include training, mentoring, and coaching, as well as experience and expectations. Employees are also attuned to perceived risks and benefits of specific actions, such as the value of wearing protective equipment and adhering to regulations. Finally, employees want to make sure they have the skills and capabilities necessary to keep them safe and that they are able to handle the physical and technical aspects of their jobs.

- *Organization.* Organizational considerations include communication with employees between units and shifts, safety and working condition policies, and compatibility with organizational goals such as choosing comfort over cost containment.

# Actions to Improve Physical Working Conditions

As with all of the RESPECT factors, actions to improve working conditions must be created or tailored to an organization. Below are some steps that may help any organization begin:

- *Spread the word about available resources.* Many organizations already have resources to supply special equipment (ergonomic computer keyboards or footstools), nursing services, safety escorts, "after-dark" taxi reimbursements, or other services. Managers must make sure employees are aware of what is available. Establishing and reinforcing emergency procedures is also essential. When problems occur, employees need to know who to call and when. Managers or designated employees should also maintain a "safety" list of employees trained in first aid or other emergency skills.

- *Prevent problems.* Prevention comes in three stages: (1) preventing problems from occurring in the first place (for example, reducing noise); (2) helping employees with existing conditions (for example, wearing earplugs); and (3) dealing with adverse effects after they arise (for example, moving an employee who has developed hearing problems). Naturally, preventing problems in the first place is the most effective, but not always possible. Effective plans should address all three problem stages.

- *Provide safety education.* Proper safety training should be provided to educate employees on what to do when things go wrong and also to highlight the consequences of inaction. Once training is completed, it's important to monitor compliance.

- *Manage the workspace.* A clean, well-ordered workspace can lead to a more efficient operation. In retail organizations, this has also been linked to reduced theft. For office workers, managers can schedule regular "purge" days during which all employees make their workspaces more efficient. The more fun the event, the greater the participation. For example, reward the employee who purged the most or showed the most "improvement."

- *Acknowledge different employee needs.* Whether it's in a cubicle bull pen or a factory floor, managers should attempt to accommodate individual differences in things like height, age, and strength. This can significantly impact how employees react to safety or environmental issues. For example, table height or minor workflow adjustments can really impact carpal tunnel syndrome or back strain.

- *Adjust the physical workplace.* Many workplaces have different "micro-climates" within the same general area. Consider adjusting the climate controls with each season. Also, make sure weekend or after-hours workers are not punished by automatic shut-offs. Brighter workspaces can deter theft and reduce eyestrain. Physical barriers between employees and customers can sometimes increase employees' feeling of security.

For example, Bobco Metals redesigned their neglected and shabby workspace and consolidated their decentralized offices into one space. This allowed management, administrative, and sales teams to interact better with each other. The design also improved the natural lighting through the addition of a longitudinal window and resulted in a stylish workplace, including a ceiling canopy made of bent and folded metal. As a result of the redesign, the company increased efficiency and operational effectiveness.[9]

# Social Working Conditions

Positive social working conditions refer primarily to teamwork and cooperation among co-workers and organizational units, and secondarily to work/life balance and work stress. It's certainly true that, in most cases, high-quality products and services do not result from the efforts of just one person. There is an interdependence of many who contribute a variety of skills, expertise, and experiences. Employees who feel they are part of a team report less stress[10] and more support in achieving work/life balance.[11]

Teamwork and cooperation are most important when groups and individuals need to rely upon each other to get things done, but that's just the beginning. It's also essential when employees are learning new skills, when they are new to an organization, and when multiple areas of expertise are required to complete an assignment. Teamwork and cooperation are also especially important when numerous employees have direct contact with customers and with self-managed teams.

---

**Barriers to Effective Teamwork and Cooperation**

When teamwork and cooperation are lacking, employees typically report:

- They are rewarded for service, but another group upon whom they rely is rewarded for efficiency; in other words, priorities may be conflicting.
- They don't know enough about how things are done to work well with co-workers.
- They don't communicate well with co-workers.
- There is not enough time to include others or to share information.
- Co-workers just pass their work along without caring how it arrives at someone else's desk.

- They are called a team but don't know what the group is aiming for or how they all fit together.
- Inflexibility on the part of the organization leads to tense, stressed team members.
- Employees are so taxed that they can't invest the time or effort to help other team members out.

# Diagnosing Problems

To improve teamwork and cooperation, identifying underlying obstacles is critical. Managers should begin by finding answers to these questions:

- Has the broader organization established and communicated a clear vision to employees? Has the organization clearly communicated how each employee and the role he or she plays fit the vision?
- Does the organization clearly state that teamwork is expected? In what ways does the organization encourage teamwork among co-workers, work groups, and other units? What example do managers set regarding this value?
- Does the organizational structure promote teamwork? For example, are interdependent work groups within the same reporting structure? Are systems in place to promote and aid cooperation and communication?
- What resources does the organization provide to support teamwork? Are there processes to facilitate communication, training, and teambuilding? Do managers have the skills and abilities to promote and support teamwork and cooperation? How do employees learn the skills to participate effectively in group decision making, problem solving, and conflict management?
- How does the organization evaluate the effectiveness of teams? In what ways does the organization recognize or reward teamwork

and cooperation? Are there shared accountabilities for success and failure? Are those who are unwilling to cooperate or join teams managed out of the system?

- If employees are working in remote locations, what effect does this have on perceptions of cooperation and fair division of labor? For such employees, how does the organization maintain the quality of communication and teamwork and align goals?

- At the time of recruiting and hiring, how does the organization evaluate a candidate's ability to work in a cooperative environment?

Managing workplace stress is important in fostering teamwork. A major contributor to stress is an imbalance between personal and professional lives—a constant nagging that, due to being stretched too thinly, personal, family, and workplace needs are not being met. To assess the stress and work/life balance support managers are offering to employees, consider the following questions:

- Are your employees visiting the doctor often? Stress has serious health consequences, such as hypertension and heart disease, depression, and alcoholism.

- Is there a sense of apathy in work groups? If stress is constant and unrelenting, employees can take on a sense of helplessness.

- Are employees quick to lose their tempers or resistant when asked to take on another project?

- How recently have the organization's policies on flexible work hours and working remotely been reviewed? Consider each job family. Is the organization making an effort to be flexible when possible?

- Are vacation and sick time policies reflective of the demands of employees' personal lives? Can employees take paid time off for caring for a sick child or family member?

- Do managers "walk the talk" when it comes to work/life balance? Are they understanding and empathetic, or do they exert minimal effort to accommodate employees' needs?

# Guiding Principles

A number of principles guide the promotion of effective teamwork and support for work/life balance and the reduction of work stress. Among the most important are

- **Provide clarity about team objectives and individual employee roles**. This is critical to gaining cooperation among members and enhancing team performance.

- **Foster trust and respect**. When trust exists among employees, communication, cooperation, and coordination of team efforts tend to be high. We all have pressures in our lives. Being understanding of others' needs will make it more likely that you will be supported when you need it.

- **Manage team size**. Smaller teams tend to show higher degrees of cooperation than larger teams. As the size of a team increases, the ability of its members to communicate and coordinate tends to decrease. Teams larger than forty members require more effort and management to maintain focus and effectiveness.

- **Team skills training**. Providing training in group decision making and conflict management improves a team's ability to adapt quickly to workplace changes and solve problems.

- **Teach managers to manage their stress**. Stress trickles down. If you have calm managers, employees are more likely to manage their work stress well.

---

### Characteristics of Effective Team Members

- Commitment to shared vision and goals
- Necessary knowledge, skills, and abilities to accomplish required tasks
- Motivation to work on the required tasks
- Skills to work as part of a team
- Encouragement of others to work as part of the team

# Actions to Improve Social Working Conditions

As with physical working conditions, effective actions to improve social working conditions depend on the issues. We believe the most effective actions to bolster teamwork and cooperation include:

- *Create understanding and share information.* Sharing may include a discussion of employee skills, abilities, talents, and work or project histories. With a smaller team, this happens more naturally, but as the size of the team increases the need for direct intervention grows. One way to share information is to include "teamwork and cooperation" as a performance measure and ask for co-worker input when it is time to evaluate performance.

- *Identify best practices.* Employees often have great ideas for improving performance. Managers can conduct sessions with co-workers doing similar jobs to learn how they accomplish their tasks. There is more than one way to accomplish most tasks. In addition, employees will gain a better understanding of the contributions of others and learn to better appreciate the value of diverse perspectives. Managers and team leaders should be on the lookout for conflicting goals within teams or larger organizations. Finally, conducting team-led interviews with the most frequently served customers can be very revealing. Employees may discover they can streamline their processes or output without diminishing their service to customers.

- *Build team spirit and goal commitment.* Annual retreats or off-site meetings underscore the importance of group efforts. These events are an excellent time to recognize and reward team accomplishments and celebrate with employees. Acknowledging milestones encourages hard work.

- *Delegate work evenly and appropriately based on skill sets.* Avoid employee burnout by spreading the work around and asking employees whether they can take on more. By asking about workload, managers avoid bottlenecks if a task gets buried on someone's to-do list (having an ever-longer to-do list is stressful in its own right). Even delegation also ensures that everyone is busy and that no one person is carrying the burden for the team. Delegating according to employees' skill sets gives them the confidence that they can excel at tasks and avoids the stress of potential failure.

# 9

# Truth

**M**ISS MAREN'S desk is in exactly the wrong place for this time of year. Beating through the windowpanes, the sun warms her arm, neck, and the right side of her face. It seems much too hot for June in Germany. Sweat beads on her forehead. "It's like an oven in here," she groans as she walks over to open the windows further.

Crank, crank, crank, with each little circular motion the window opens a bit more. She grimaces at the size of the opening. She doesn't know why she bothers; there's no breeze today anyway, and even if there were, the wind couldn't find its way up and through that miniscule horizontal slat. Resigned to sweltering, she sits down again, her sweat acting like an adhesive between the back of her knees and her vinyl chair. The only thing cool about her classroom is the blackboard. For a brief moment she thinks about pressing her hot forehead against it.

If the sun weren't flushing her face, her blood pressure would be. Her job is becoming increasingly difficult. As far as she can tell, each year it is the same rhetoric. The state government bemoans budget shortfalls and gives indications of bigger class sizes and lean times ahead. The teachers' union responds in kind, claiming the quality of education is at stake. Each side of the debate takes its case to the ridiculous extreme, painting a dramatic rendition of the situation. However, usually a sensible agreement is struck over the summer and adequate resources are allocated.

This year, though, the union has its work cut out. The budget deficit is real, and citizens know it. There is little doubt that class sizes will remain large and the number of teacher positions few. The question is: Will there be additional reductions in positions? Will class sizes get even *larger?*

There's little information to go on, so Maren fears the worst. The Ministry of Education has been talking in platitudes, acknowledging the shortfall but stopping short of saying exactly which part of the deficit will be rectified through budget cuts. School administrators have taken a different approach and remain largely silent; this tactic is even more unnerving. Similarly, the headmaster has absolutely no information to share that can quell others' fears; everyone is worried about the effects of a too-lean staff on students' learning. The lack of information from local education administrators is, frankly, shocking.

"How am I supposed to teach when the classroom is filled to capacity?" she wonders. She worries about her effectiveness next year. She thinks she has done well at her job; her classroom is largely in control and her kids have learned the curriculum. On the other hand, it seemed as if the headmaster was checking in more than usual. Was that coincidence? Cuts from the previous year increased her class size, and at times she had felt like a glorified babysitter to thirty-two seven-year-olds.

As she ponders her fate, worry morphs into anger. For someone who gets true joy from watching her students learn, it is painful to watch a budget crisis get in the way of their success—and hers. She knows how to teach, but doesn't know how to be effective under these conditions. "If they are going to cut the budget, maybe they could tell us how to teach under such ridiculous circumstances!"

# Telling the Truth

It doesn't matter whether an employee is a teacher like Maren, a butcher, a baker, or a candlestick maker; employees build relationships based on trust, and you can't have trust without honesty.[1,2] Ten percent of employees said the most important thing they wanted from their organizations was truth in communication. For employees, communication is broken into three categories: honest information from management, performance feedback, and, simply, better communication in general (see Figure 9.1).

**Figure 9.1. Truthful Communication Employees Want**

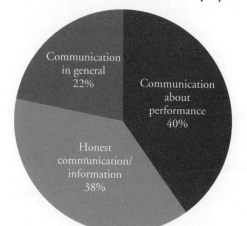

Looking more closely at employees' comments, we see truthfulness reoccurring as a theme. There is also an emphasis on access to information and the open exchange of information, including management's efforts to listen to employees' opinions. Some typical employee comments about workplace truthfulness include:

- "Clear definition of goals"
- "Truthfulness from managers and leaders"
- "For management to say what they mean and to mean what they say"

- "To know that the company is financially viable and can withstand economic ups and downs"
- "Feedback—good or bad; a person needs to know whether he's doing his job properly and in what areas he can improve. Better access to the answers and decisions I need to do my job better"
- "To value the workers' ideas and to keep us informed on all work matters"
- "Open communication and transparency"

# Is Maren Receiving the Communication and Feedback She Needs?

Maren's first source of concern is the lack of information from top management in her case. Less than half of employees like Maren—women in the education industry in Europe—report open, two-way communication and feel they can believe what management says. In both cases, the perception of the honesty in senior leaders' communication lags behind the global average.

Maren's grievances don't end there. Not only does she have a hazy picture of the challenges faced by her industry and the role layoffs might play, but she doesn't have the information she needs to adjust her performance in the wake of budget cuts. Sixty-two percent of employees like Maren believe that they have fair performance evaluations, and that beats the international average of 57 percent. However, when we asked who has actually *had* a performance evaluation in that last twelve months, only 53 percent of people like Maren have had one (the global average is 58 percent). The most glaring problem these data reveal is that more than two of every five employees aren't even being evaluated and therefore have little hope of improving.

## The Management Credibility Gap

Employees' frustrations with the lack of transparency from senior leadership can be encapsulated in a single survey respondent's comment: "Don't lie to me. Don't lay off my staff members without consulting me.

Don't tell us the company made $17 million then tell me the next day that I can't give bonuses or raises to my staff because the stockholders are more important than the employees."

Ouch. Particularly during times of economic duress, both employees and managers feel pressure to make the right decisions for themselves and for their team members. To make good decisions, employees need accurate and timely information. If there is an informational vacuum, the pressure leads to anger, resentment, and distrust. If you want your organization to escape this vicious cycle of discontent, then consider the old adage: "The truth can set you free."

It may come as a shock to management, but most employees do not believe their managers or company leaders. Leaders can't be effective if their employees don't believe them; previous research has demonstrated that transparency is related to leadership effectiveness.[3,4] Forty-nine percent of employees in the United States agreed with the statement, "When my company's senior management says something, you can believe it's true." Believe it or not, this is a major improvement from the historical low point in 1990, when only 31 percent believed their senior leaders (see Figure 9.2).

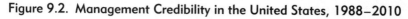

**Figure 9.2. Management Credibility in the United States, 1988–2010**

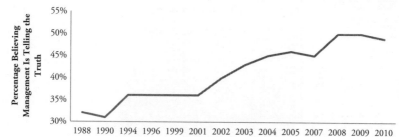

# Trickle-Down Information

While it's true that employees today are more apt to believe messages from the C-suite than they were twenty years ago, what messages are being conveyed? Are employees receiving the information they need to make decisions about their work, careers, and livelihood?

It is leaders' responsibility, after all, to ensure that information is shared with employees and to be role models for creating a culture of candor.[5] People use messages from managers to judge the health of the organization and decide whether to stay or go. Information about the company's direction influences everything from employee commitment on specific projects to their general ongoing commitment to the organization. Employees make the choice to stay every day, so information must be regular. This isn't just idle speculation: if employees agreed that their leaders conveyed a clear direction for the company, 91 percent also agreed that they knew how their work fit into the goals of the organization. If no direction was visible, only 64 percent understood how their jobs contributed to the company's success or failure.

There's also an employee-management disconnect when it comes to information. While 67 percent know where the organization is headed, the converse is frightening—33 percent of executives cannot claim to have a clear picture of their company's direction (see Figure 9.3). That's one-third of executives who simply don't know where the organization is going and therefore have no hope of providing that information to their employees.

**Figure 9.3. Knowing the Direction the Organization Is Headed: Global Job Type Comparison**

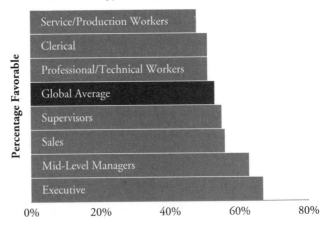

We would call that a major problem. How would you explain it? It's possible that leadership simply doesn't have the skills to lead the company. Or it could be a result of a culture of secrecy or just incredibly poor communication. Regardless of the reason, not only are ill-informed leaders making decisions on supposition and guesswork, but they are also unable to share information with their business units simply because they don't have the information to share. When leaders don't know where the organization is going, everyone is in the dark.

The number of employees who understand the direction of the organization decreases as we travel down the corporate ladder. It is akin to the child's game "telephone," where children sit in a circle, and the first child whispers a phrase to a neighbor. The whispered message is passed from child to child, around the circle. By journey's end, the message is mangled and its original meaning is unrecognizable. So it often is with organizational communication. By the time information hits first-line supervisors—those charged with delivering information to the workforce at-large—only 55 percent report that senior management has conveyed a clear organizational path. It grows worse from there, with only 48 percent of service and production workers aware of their organization's charted course.

# Delivering Honest Feedback

Honesty starts at the top, and what is said must be translated into something that improves the performance of an organization. The direction a company takes should be reflected in employees' goals, and each employee's performance on the job should be aligned with that direction. Job performance feedback—the information an employee receives about how he or she is doing on the job—is how employees know to what extent they have been successful at helping the organization move forward toward its goals.

Often, we think of feedback as the information shared with an employee during a performance appraisal. This doesn't provide a complete picture. We also think of feedback as recognition, which we covered in Chapter 3. Again, that is only part of the picture. Feedback is provided to us almost every minute of every day. Unhappy bosses scowl; our audience gives blank faces if the message isn't clear; computers beep if we push the wrong button; an assembly line shuts down if quality checks aren't met; and a delivery is logged as late if the warehouse fails to supply inventory. These cues are all feedback. As employees, we take all of this information and adjust how we perform on the job. Without feedback, no change can occur and performance cannot be improved.

It is up to HR and management to pull this information together and present it in a fair and accurate way. This often means supplementing hard metrics, such as quality measures or sales revenue generated with "softer" metrics—information that speaks to how a person interacts with others to get work done. Often, the feedback based on softer metrics is missing or, if available, perceived by the employee as inaccurate. Just 59 percent of the international group of employees we surveyed report that their managers supply them with useful feedback. While employees like Maren are more likely to have performance evaluations, they are slightly less likely to have the benefit of their managers' feedback. Evaluations without useful, ongoing performance feedback not only can be counterproductive, but can be downright unsettling to employees. It makes performance appraisals, at best, seem like a box to be checked on the managerial to-do list and, at worst, a downright scary event for employees—truly a missed opportunity.

## Feedback for High Potentials

There is a strong argument to be made that all employees deserve performance feedback. Not only does it demonstrate that employees are worthy of managerial time and effort, but it gives them a shot at improving their work—and that is certainly in the organization's best interest. Another argument, from a pragmatic perspective, is that organizations should focus the limited amount of time, energy, and financial resources they have on the development of the most promising employees—the "high potentials."

At a minimum we would expect those enrolled in management development programs to receive consistent feedback as they prepare to move up the management ladder. While only about half of all employees receive performance appraisals and feedback, approximately 75 percent of high-potential employees do. At first glance that seems like encouraging news for these high potentials, but that leaves a substantial chunk—25 percent—without a clear indication of what they're doing right or wrong (see Figure 9.4). Without performance feedback for high potentials, the investment made in their development may be wasted.

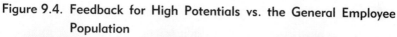

**Figure 9.4. Feedback for High Potentials vs. the General Employee Population**

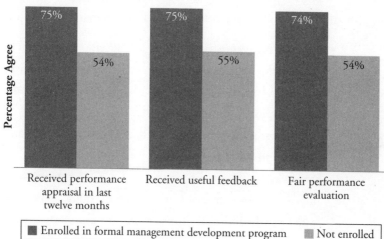

Call feedback the gateway to development. When delivered properly, it provides individuals with the motivation to learn and improve. In the absence of feedback, employees make up their own truths. They may underestimate their abilities and commit to lower goals. They might be overconfident and, with the vacuum of information on their performance, fail. Either way, the goals and performance of employees are not supporting the mission, direction, and goals of the organization.

# Opening the Lines of Communication and Telling the Truth

Honest communication starts at the top. Leaders model it and employees follow suit; this improves everyone's performance.[6] Highly skilled leadership teams share a common vision and create a clear picture of the organization's future so that managers and employees can execute targeted goals. Whether the message is about organizational strategy or individual performance, credible and helpful communication is required. This includes addressing challenges and plans that have been made for achieving goals. Employees must also see plans as achievable, trusting leaders enough to feel good about following them.

Employees must believe their leaders are honest. A number of key contributors to employee perceptions of leaders being truthful are

- *Compelling vision.* Effective leaders develop visions that motivate employees. The vision needs to enlist employees to contribute to its fulfillment. Consistency of vision helps employees develop a sense of trust in the organization.
- *Alignment among leaders.* It's bad when employees in different parts of an organization hear different or conflicting messages about an organization's future. Aniisu K. Verghese, the head of internal communications at Sapient in India, believes trust in leadership is declining. Employees, he says, particularly India's workforce between the ages of twenty-three and twenty-five, expect leaders to be hands-on, to be open to feedback, and to take direct responsibility for their actions. They want to be included in decision making and to be kept informed. To build trust, Verghese recommends starting with transparent communication and making sure managers are strategically aligned.[7]
- *Consistent behavior.* Consistency builds credibility. Integrity is doing what you said you were going to do. When leaders do this, employees see them as trustworthy. Employees watch carefully to see whether leaders' espoused philosophy is the same

as their practice. For example, the organization may profess to value work/life balance, yet leaders demonstrate "workaholic" behaviors and, worse, expect the same from direct reports. Such contradictions do not build a culture of trust.

- *Success.* When leaders communicate goals, align resources for their achievement, and actually meet or exceed them, the more credible they are and the more truthful they appear. Employees are more likely to achieve their goals and deliver expected results when they trust their leaders.

# Diagnosing Your Organization's Culture of Truthfulness

If employees have concerns about whether their leaders are telling the truth, organizations should ask themselves some questions, including:

- What have leaders done to provide employees with more visible, credible leadership? What opportunities have leaders taken to engage in direct conversations or Q&A sessions with employees?
- What can middle and lower-level managers do to clarify and reinforce messages from higher levels? What are middle and lower-level managers doing to build trust and credibility?
- Can employees provide information to leaders without fear of retribution? What mechanisms are in place to facilitate this? What is the track record for responding to employee questions and concerns?
- What methods does the organization use to communicate its vision, mission, values, and progress? Do middle and lower-level managers have access to communication aids to help them convey important information?
- How do employees decide how well the organization is managed? Is it through publicly available information? Is it based only on observation? How visible have senior leaders been to employees, and what types of contact have been made?

---

**Common Communication Mistakes When Building a Culture of Truthfulness**

- *Waiting too long.* Leaders may be waiting to communicate about important developments or changes until "all the details are ironed out." As a result, employees are probably hearing misinformation "through the grapevine." By the time leaders get around to communicating, it may be too late because opinions about the subject have already been formed.
- *Over-reliance on the chain of command.* The organization may be relying too much on communication down the "chain of command." Important messages may be reaching lower levels in a garbled or confusing form, or perhaps not at all.
- *Lack of repetition.* The organization may be announcing important information only once, and then assuming awareness and understanding on everyone's part. Any message worth hearing is worth repeating.
- *Lack of access.* The organization may be relying on the use of corporate communication vehicles (internal website, email, newsletters, etc.) that are not, in fact, accessible to, or even read by, all employees. In addition, these vehicles may have their own production schedule, which causes information to be late, lost, or useless.
- *Over-emphasizing the positive.* Negative messages are hard to deliver, whether at an organizational level or to individual employees about their performance. Truthful communication is balanced and includes the positive and negative sides of issues.

---

# Guiding Principles for Building a Culture of Truthfulness

In building a culture of truthfulness, leaders and managers have unique responsibilities. In smaller organizations, these responsibilities may all reside at the same level of management.

### Promoting Trust in Senior Leaders

- *Make senior leaders visible*. People have to be known to be trusted. Middle and lower-level managers have to make it easier for senior leaders to be visible to employees. Access can help senior leaders gain credibility.

  At Sony Pictures, based in Culver City, California, with 6,300 employees worldwide, company leaders initiated an effort to provide more transparency, openness, and trust between themselves and their teams. Each team member committed to actively participate in discussions and make decisions based on the good of the company, instead of furthering his or her individual needs.[8]

- *Present a balanced picture*. Over-emphasizing the positive and ignoring challenges can damage an organization's credibility. Give employees the full picture.

  AT HCL Technologies in India, the 360-reviews of senior leaders are accessible to all employees on the firm's intranet site. The goal is to provide more transparency and empowerment and ultimately encourage managers to better support their employees. In addition, the company CEO spends an average of seven hours a week responding directly to complaints or questions that employees submit though their service desk. His responses are also posted on the company intranet.[9]

- *Help front-line employees see the world from management's eyes*. Running an organization is hard work, and difficult choices are being made all the time. The more managers share what goes into their decisions, the more likely the entire organization will have a unified commitment and sense of purpose.

  In 2010 SAS received the Great Places to Work Institute's award for being the number one company to work for in America. For the second year in a row, they also topped *Fortune* magazine's list of "100 Best Companies to Work For." The firm develops analytical software systems for companies worldwide. Employees at SAS trust their leadership because messages from leaders are reinforced by their actions. Employees report they are confident of long-term success, and 98 percent indicate the company is often or almost always a great place to work. To improve transparency and trust, SAS leadership has recently implemented several initiatives to bolster communication. In addition to candid question-and-answer sessions, leaders have started blogging with and participating in live webcasts to their global staff. These initiatives help provide open, honest, and transparent leadership and have contributed to the firm's low rate of employee turnover, high number of job applicants, excellent customer service, and financial success.[10]

**Promoting Trust in Middle and Lower-Level Managers**

- *Share rationale.* When possible, share the rationale for high-level decisions. Employees' trust is higher when they understand why decisions are made.
- *Provide solid performance information.* In order for performance feedback to be deemed "accurate" by employees, it needs to be collected from credible sources and, whenever possible, be based on hard numbers. Leaders should set up data collection, management, and reporting systems that make performance data accessible and accurate.

## HOW'S YOUR CREDIBILITY?

Leadership credibility is essential for an organization's success. When leaders communicate information accurately, offer their rationale for decisions, and allow an open exchanges of ideas, they are more likely to be viewed as trustworthy.

Also, when leaders and managers demonstrate concern for the welfare of others (for example, acting on behalf of employee interests or demonstrating sensitivity to employee concerns), they are more likely to be trusted.

Finally, when leaders demonstrate consistency and integrity in all their interactions with employees, their credibility is enhanced.

# Actions to Build a Culture of Truthfulness

Which actions that your company undertakes will depend on diagnosing your organization's current state. These eight ideas can help you start:

- **Keep employees updated.** Ensure that employees are regularly informed about how the organization is doing against its key objectives. Communicate key operational and financial results regularly and in a way employees can understand.

  Consider the experience of Skyline Construction. When two of the owners left the company, the commercial construction firm based in San Francisco allowed its employees to purchase their shares. This shift in ownership significantly impacted the level of transparency and sharing of information. Today, the company's financial information is shared regularly, and decisions are made collaboratively, with employees involved in developing solutions to problems. Due to the new leadership approach, employees have become more team-oriented, particularly noticeable during the recent recession, when the company was forced to lay off more than a dozen employees. In order to prevent additional layoffs, employees volunteered to take a 10 percent reduction in pay. Half of the pay cut was later repaid.[11]

- **Provide an upward communication system.** Create formal mechanisms, such as an employee engagement survey, for employees to share their ideas. Keep in mind that what an organization chooses to measure sends a message about its values. At Lincoln Electric they have an open door policy that has been in place for decades and allows all employees to speak directly to the CEO.[12]

- **Share performance feedback regularly.** If feedback is delivered in small doses, employees can make small corrections throughout the year. This avoids a difficult, annual conversation about how an employee has demonstrated sub-par performance, which leads to resentment. If all employees, whether bosses, direct reports, or peers, share feedback with each other in a casual, non-confrontational way, the path to performance improvement is far easier.

- *Make sure information spreads across the organization.* Senior leaders should realize the importance of being visible two or more levels down. They should visit lower-level work groups and help package information for lower-level managers to pass along to employees.

- *Conduct town hall meetings.* Often held every three to six months, these events allow leaders to present new directions, take questions, and build confidence that the truth is being told. Senior leaders can also use informal discussions—over lunch, for example—as a way to increase two-way dialogue, visibility, and a culture of truthfulness.

- *Encourage upward communication within the management ranks.* Middle- and lower-level managers should create opportunities to discuss the leadership climate with their own managers; these conversations should include concerns about leadership's ability or credibility.

Virginia Blood Services, a Richmond-based non-profit organization, uses leadership development to teach managers how to build trust with their employees. The twelve-week program begins with all participants taking part in a 360-degree feedback review to help them identify areas of weakness and opportunity.[13]

# 10

# RESPECT: A Key to Your Future Success

**I**T SOUNDS ALMOST like a cliché to say it, but these are dramatic, exciting, and fast-moving times. The people who make up an organization—CEOs, senior executives, managers, and front-line employees—are all devising ways to stay afloat or, better yet, thrive amid the ebb and flow of globalization and technology. Those producing cars, televisions, business services, pharmaceuticals, technology—you name it—all face global competition. Even businesses and professions once thought to be immune are having their assumptions turned upside down. Consider your well-paid local doctor. Today, high-quality licensed physicians in India are reading digitized CAT scans, MRIs, and x-rays from patients around the world. Every product and service seemingly is up for grabs.

Companies that innovate have a strong competitive edge, but just barely. Consider the challenges facing Apple Computer, the company that essentially created an entirely new technology category with its iPad. Less than a year later, dozens of name-brand competitors are offering their own tablet computers. The innovative edge—the ability to innovate time and time again—comes from an organization's ability to flex and adapt to the environment; it comes from the ability to do away with highly bureaucratic structures and move toward a more dynamic organization.

For leaders to shift their organization's structure from bureaucratic to dynamic, embedding RESPECT in their culture and practices is a condition that *must* be met. We'll talk more about making that paradigm shift later in this chapter, but the concept is important because, as the world changes, so do customers, requiring organizations to be increasingly responsive. Customers have become incredibly sophisticated, knowledgeable, and vocal about their needs. An organization's ability to be flexible depends, without a doubt, on employees' commitment to the organization, their motivation to stick with it even in times of change, and the knowledge and skills to make it all work. RESPECT ensures that employees are up to the challenge.

Throughout this book we've shared the research and knowledge we've learned from over twenty-five years of studying employees and their organizations. We've been able to conclusively link employee satisfaction and engagement to customer satisfaction and business performance. Organizations that provide their employees with the seven fundamental elements of *RESPECT*—*Recognition*, *Exciting work*, *Security* of employment, fair *Pay*, *Education and career growth*, high-quality workplace *Conditions*, and *Truth* in the form of honest communication—outperform their peers. To survive and thrive in the future, we believe that many organizations must undergo a fundamental paradigm shift in their organizational style, switching from bureaucratic to dynamic. And as you'll see, you can't have a dynamic organization without RESPECT.

Lip service alone won't do the trick. Its commonplace for leaders to say their organizations are evolving, but inside the company walls it is often business as usual. We call this M&M management—after those tasty chocolate candies—because you can change the color of an M&M's candy shell, but inside it's still the same chocolate.

# The Leadership-Employee RESPECT Disconnect

It's a fun name, but M&M management is a real phenomenon that we've witnessed through our years of surveying leaders, managers, and employees. Leaders like to talk about radical changes and employee-centric practices, but, in fact, there's a strong disconnect between how leaders perceive their organization's RESPECT levels and how their employees view them.

When we asked senior executives whether their organization provides the elements of RESPECT, 69 percent of them said "yes." When we asked the same thing of individual contributors (non-management), only 52 percent of them agreed (see Figure 10.1). This exposes a seventeen percentage point gap between how leaders believe their organizations behave and how employees view the situation. One way to look at this is that conditions for management are pretty good—they are getting most of what they need from the company—and the conditions for non-management, well, they're not nearly as good. It could also signal that leaders simply don't have a feel for what's going on in the trenches. In all reality, it is probably a bit of both: organizational practices and policies cater to management, and management doesn't have a realistic picture of employees' needs.

Either way it's a bad-for-business gap, and it exists in every element of our RESPECT index. You probably won't be surprised to learn the discrepancy exists when it comes to pay, with 63 percent of senior leaders reporting they are fairly paid, compared to only 47 percent for non-management. What may be surprising, however, is that the two biggest management-employee RESPECT disconnects—nineteen percentage points each—have to do with Excitement and Truth in the workplace. Seventy-six percent of senior leaders find excitement in their work, compared with just 57 percent for non-management employees. When it comes to truth, we asked whether statements by senior leaders are credible, and only 66 percent of executives agreed. Think about that for a moment: that means a full third of senior leaders don't believe the truthfulness of the public statements coming from their own leadership teams. It shouldn't be a surprise then that only 45 percent of non-management employees believe these executives.

---

**Figure 10.1. Comparison of RESPECT Index Scores for Senior Leaders and Individual Contributors (Non-Management)**

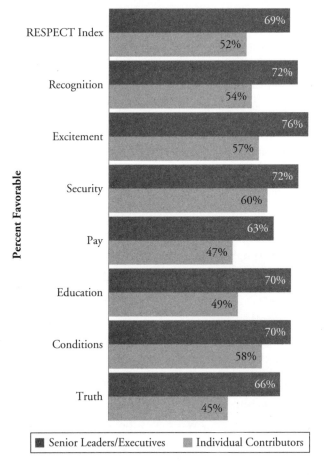

| | Senior Leaders/Executives | Individual Contributors |

Indeed, employees are hard to fool. They have keen instincts and insights when it comes to their companies and, we believe, they often provide a more realistic snapshot. The picture looks like this: senior leaders—those who run business units—believe they are managing in a progressive way that's good for business. Yet, when you ask the rest of the company what they think, their opinion is that the new boss feels a whole lot like the old boss.

The evidence for the M&M management disconnect is strong. Too many people are working in organizations in which leaders think they are progressive, but in fact are not. Deluded about the environment they've created for their employees, leaders aren't being realistic about the structures and processes in which employees work. This disconnect is the single biggest obstacle holding back organizations' transformation from being bureaucratic to being dynamic.

So what to do about it? First, leaders must understand what separates a bureaucratic organization from a dynamic one. Then they can start applying solutions.

## The Bureaucratic Organization

Bureaucracies[1] can be difficult to navigate and slow to respond, but in some situations they work quite well. Before the dawn of technology, industry was built methodically. The business and market environments moved slowly; they were subject to evolution, not revolution. Organizations built strength through consistency and having a few smart people make all of the important decisions. Big producers of goods did one or two things, and they did them with great success The standardization of products and services allowed organizations to scale quickly, reduce costs, generate profits, and satisfy mass needs. Their standard policies and centralized decision making worked well in very stable environments and managed unskilled workforces efficiently.

However, in today's world, not allowing employees to make decisions can lead to serious consequences. Often, these are the companies that have rules that make little sense in the real world, but employees must follow them or risk demotion or being fired. These are the organizations in which customers must scream at the top of their lungs for a manager before anything is done to solve a problem. Employees would like to help, but rules are rules and they have little latitude to fix things that are broken. Although "functional bureaucracies" can survive for a long time, that doesn't mean that they are thriving. Large organizations do need rules and guidelines, but they also must be able to adapt to fluid situations.

In our ever-changing, dynamic environment, we need organizations that match the pace of change. Rarely will bureaucratic organizations perform at the level of their more dynamic peers. The first sign of bureaucratic organizations is power and intellect highly concentrated in the top echelon. Problems aren't solved on the front lines where they occur, but in the executive suite. After the leadership team comes up with a solution, a mandate is sent down through the ranks to be carried out. These companies often use silos that bring with them complex territorial issues whereby one unit's success might be at the expense of another. Turf wars are not uncommon. Front-line employees at these firms tend to have simple jobs that are mapped out for them by an executive they've most likely never met. A manager's job tends to be focused on implementation, monitoring, motivation, and control over others. Not to be too flippant, but if you took out the motivation you could apply the same management roles to jail wardens.

Stable business environments are becoming a thing of the past, and that means these sorts of bureaucracies are at risk. As consumers become increasingly sophisticated, they could lose patience with the slow response of functional bureaucracies and turn to the competition. Bureaucratic silos also make it hard to handle customers (*I'm sorry, let me transfer you to the department that can help you*). The lack of cooperation between business units stifles teamwork and innovation. That means it's left to those in the executive suite to offer solutions. In stable times that might be manageable, but in dynamic times the executive suite can become overloaded and overwhelmed. You can almost see a firm's intellectual gears seizing up as it tries to adjust.

# The Dynamic Organization

If bureaucratic organizations are defined by their top-down structure and stable environment, a dynamic organization is active, with a focus squarely on the power of the front-line managers and employees to solve problems. In bureaucracies, interactions between company and customer have often been scripted out *ad nauseam*. Yet, in the real world we know that it's impossible to map out every contingency. Things change; customer needs evolve and so do their problems.

Leadership focus at a dynamic organization isn't on command and control, but on empowerment and participation by employees. Unlike the simple jobs that are assigned to their peers in bureaucracies, the jobs of employees at dynamic organizations are increasingly more challenging and complex. A manager at a dynamic organization must motivate employees, but also identify and promote opportunities that allow employees to thrive.

Dynamic organizations are expert at forming cross-functional teams in which employees are encouraged to contribute and to offer solutions to problems. The manager's job with such a team isn't to assert authority but to spur smart, creative solutions and make sure employees are contributing at the highest level and living up to their best potential. Team members are also learning new skills from their cross-functional counterparts, and this interchange often leads to new innovation. Our research shows that cross-functional teams also make employees more committed to their jobs. It's the opposite of a bureaucratic silo. Dynamic organizations thrive because they give their employees the latitude and flexibility to adapt and solve novel problems on the spot without having to run every item up to the C-suite

Flexibility is a key competitive advantage of a dynamic organization. Flexibility also applies to where and when the actual work takes place. Leaders of dynamic organizations emphasize the quality of work and, when practical, de-emphasize the actual physical space where it's carried out. Some jobs require employees to be at their desks from 9 to 5, but others don't, and dynamic organizations empower those employees to work where they are most efficient. Some days this might be at home, and some days this might be during non-traditional work hours. This type of flexibility empowers employees and amplifies their feelings of RESPECT. This in turn helps organizations perform at higher levels. A dynamic strategy allows organizations to focus on satisfying their customers and to evolve along with their customers' needs.

Shifting from a bureaucratic to a dynamic organization is no small order. Indeed, we believe part of the leadership-employee disconnect we identified at the beginning of this chapter reflects the struggle some companies have with the transformation.

## Do's and Don'ts for RESPECT

Every organization is unique, with its own culture and history, but some fundamental "do's" that dynamic organizations use to keep their employees engaged are listed in Table 10.1. There are also some fundamental "don'ts" that bureaucratic organizations use that tend to alienate employees. Table 10.1 is by no means a comprehensive list, but it will start you thinking in the right way.

## Dynamic Organizations and the Coming War for Talent

The recent recession and its high unemployment rates have lulled many business leaders into believing there is a glut of talent, but as the global economy continues to improve, organizations are going to face stiff competition for qualified employees. In August 2009, in the midst of the recent Great Recession, *The Wall Street Journal* reported that, despite a 9.5 percent unemployment rate in the United States, several industries were having a very difficult time filling skilled positions.[2] Now that things seem to be improving, finding high-quality talent will only become more difficult. In March of 2011, for example, the research and consulting firm Bersin and Associates issued a report entitled Global Growth Creates a New War for Talent. The Bersin study showed that, for the first

**Table 10.1. The Do's and Don'ts of Delivering RESPECT**

| RESPECT Category | Don't | Don't | Do | Do | Do |
|---|---|---|---|---|---|
| *Recognition* | Ignore employee performance until the annual review. | Focus only on criticism. | Close the gap between employee actions and the time those actions are recognized. | Explain how specific employee actions led to specific outcomes. | Make informal recognition a habit. |
| *Exciting work* | Give employees a specific job so they master one assignment and only one assignment. | Keep your employees in the dark about company initiatives and strategy. Allow them to focus solely on their jobs. | Provide variety. Employees who can develop and deploy a wide range of skills are more satisfied at work. | Discuss with employees what they do and don't like about their jobs. It's the only way you'll know. | Have fun! Group social activities promote group interaction and teamwork, and they add variety to the day. |
| *Security* | Share information only with C-level executives, believing the less the rank-and-file know, the better it is. | Limit training and development with existing employees, believing they'll only leave once they acquire more skills. | Invest time, energy, and money in employee training and development—you'll outperform the competition. | Engage in formal workforce forecasting and planning. Be proactive, not reactive. | Create a flexible work environment in which employees have a say in how they work—the trust will empower them and ease concern about their roles. |
| *Pay* | Hide key benefits from employees with the hope they won't use them, based on the mistaken notion that this saves money. | Make compensation structures and decisions opaque in the hopes that employees will assume they are fair. | Create an annual compensation and benefits review. Many employees don't realize everything that's available to them. | Acknowledge a job well done. Psychological rewards can compensate for lower pay. | Give deserving employees a day off. It's a cost-effective and highly appreciated reward. |

*(Continued)*

**Table 10.1. (Continued)**

| RESPECT Category | Don't | Do | Do | Do |
|---|---|---|---|---|
| *Education and career growth* | Silo employees and units so they can specialize in one area. | Make employees take the initiative when it comes to training. | Cross-train employees. They'll learn new skills, thereby increasing excitement and job security. | Establish and use a training budget, and factor time away from the job into the analysis. | Hold formal and (at least) annual career discussions with employees to learn their goals and aspirations. |
| *Conditions* | Increase worker stress by increasing workload, assuming higher levels of productivity result from longer hours. | Play favorites with employees as a means to pit team members against each other. | Be clear about team and individual roles and objectives on specific projects. | Limit team size. Groups larger than forty tend to lose focus and are difficult to manage. | Listen to employee complaints about their physical environment and follow health and safety guidelines. |
| *Truth* | Avoid telling employees the full story, even when things are bad and you fear it will make them nervous and less productive. | Keep a closed-door policy so executives don't have to answer frivolous and distracting questions from employees. | Create a balanced picture of your organization's health. Employees know when things are bad. Lying about it only undermines credibility. | Regularly discuss strategic issues with employees. Use town hall events or smaller team-based meetings. | Include employees in goal-setting exercises. Increased involvement builds trust and commitment. |

time in three years, more than half of all business leaders stated that their businesses was being *held back* by a lack of talent. While Western Europe and the United States are still emerging from the recession, Bersin reported that companies in parts of Eastern Europe, China, and India are already seeing revenue jump by as much as 30 percent.[3]

"We are re-entering a marketplace in which talent will play a vital role," said Josh Bersin, the firm's chief executive. "As businesses have shifted their priorities to focus on new product introductions, growth, and acceleration in hiring, HR organizations are focusing on programs to encourage innovation, increase employee engagement, and drive individual performance."

Organizations will have to be dynamic to compete in the global economy and to win the coming talent war. To be truly dynamic, organizations have to fully embrace the principles of RESPECT. The elements that make an organization dynamic are in fact the same ones that create RESPECT in the workplace. The two are inextricably linked. At the risk of being redundant, you simply can't have a dynamic organization without RESPECT. A dynamic organization provides a flexible workplace with challenging and empowering jobs—and that's just what employees want.

> "To find out what one is fitted to do, and to secure an opportunity to do it, is the key to happiness."
>
> *—John Dewey*

> "Far and away the best prize that life has to offer is the chance to work hard at work worth doing."
>
> *—Theodore Roosevelt*

> "All labor that uplifts humanity has dignity and importance and should be undertaken with painstaking excellence."
>
> *—Dr. Martin Luther King*

# A

# Identifying RESPECT Levels Worksheet

*C***ALLING ALL DATA!** In this appendix, we offer a method
for reviewing your data at a high level to help you understand
where your organization might need improvement in RESPECT. After
completing this exercise and reading the respective chapters, you might
decide to analyze the relevant pieces of data further or collect additional
data to pinpoint the specific issues within your organization.

See the chart on the following pages.

| | Definition | Questions to Answer | Potential Sources of Data | Our Organization's Data-Based Answers |
|---|---|---|---|---|
| Recognition | A pat on the back from managers and the organization at-large | Do managers coach, support, and encourage their direct reports? Is recognition embedded in the culture? Are our recognition programs used, and are employees "gaming the system"? Does the leadership team value each employee's contribution? | Performance measurement systems Multi-rater scores Recognition program usage Employee engagement survey | |
| Exciting work | A job that's challenging, interesting, and fun | Does each person's job utilize his or her talents to the utmost? Do all employees have a strong reason why they work? Do employees set goals they care about? What percentage of employee goals is reached? | Employee engagement survey Exit survey Goal-setting system Multi-rater data analyzed for development needs | |

| Security | Job security, whether that means for one year or ten | What does "job security" mean to employees? | Employee engagement survey |
| | | Are workers afraid of layoffs? | Confidential focus groups |
| | | For how long do employees expect to be able to work at your organization? | Turnover rates and job tenure |
| | | How long should they expect to be employed? | |
| Pay | Fair compensation for a day's work, and enough of it | Are people with the same job and responsibilities being paid similarly? | Payroll + HRIS |
| | | Does your organization have pay inequities between men and women? | Compensation survey |
| | | | Job market value research |
| | | Do employees have an accurate understanding of what is "fair pay" in the marketplace and at your organization? | Employee opinion survey for perceptions of fair pay |
| | | Is each employee paid fairly? | |

(Continued)

| | Definition | Questions to Answer | Potential Sources of Data | Our Organization's Data-Based Answers |
|---|---|---|---|---|
| Education and career growth | Opportunities to develop skills and career advancement | What are the development needs of certain groups of employees, such as management?<br><br>What remedial development do under-performing or recently promoted employees need?<br><br>Does every employee have a next career step planned within your organization?<br><br>Do employees know what skills they need to develop to take the next step?<br><br>What skills do your high-potential employees need to reach your organization's expectations?<br><br>Are they properly trained to be successful in their jobs? | Multi-rater scores<br><br>Performance appraisals<br><br>Talent management system<br><br>Succession management system<br><br>Employee development plans<br><br>Employee engagement survey | |
| Conditions | A workplace that is comfortable physically and socially, and well-equipped | Is there a sense of teamwork throughout the organization, and if not, what groups come up short? | Employee opinion survey<br><br>Direct reports' ratings of managers on multi-rater surveys | |

| | Questions | Tools |
|---|---|---|
| | Do managers treat their direct reports respectfully, acknowledging their expertise and saving criticism for a private conversation? | Work plan and staffing analysis |
| | Are there enough people on staff to do the priority projects? | Occupational safety audit |
| | Is the workplace safe for all employees? | |
| | Do occupational conditions meet regulations, or better yet, exceed them? | |
| **Truth**<br>Frank, honest, and transparent leaders | What rumors are circulating about the decisions made at the top? | Employee opinion survey |
| | How much do line employees know about the organization's plan for the future? | Goal-setting system |
| | Does each employee know how his or her work aligns to organizational goals? | Performance appraisal system |
| | Do employees receive timely, honest feedback, both positive and negative, about their performance? | Multi-rater scores |
| | | Balanced scorecard |

# B

# About the WorkTrends Study

**T**HE WORKTRENDS STUDY has collected and researched the opinions of workers from a random selection of full-time employees in the United States nearly every year since 1945. Employees who are over eighteen years old and work full-time at an organization larger than one hundred employees may take the WorkTrends survey. The survey is comprehensive, with more than 120 questions that ask employees about workplace issues, such as managerial and leadership effectiveness, training and development, satisfaction with compensation, diversity practices, turnover intention, and job satisfaction. Additional questions ask about organizational phenomena, such as incidence of layoffs or mergers and acquisitions. Demographic questions are also included, such as gender, age, job type, industry, and organizational size.

Since 2007, WorkTrends has been administered online, allowing data to be collected outside of the United States. In 2010, approximately ten thousand workers in the United States and one thousand individuals in each of the following countries/regions took the survey online: Australia, Brazil, Canada, China, Denmark, Finland, France, Germany, India, Italy, Japan, Mexico, The Netherlands, Russia, Spain, Sweden, Switzerland, the United Kingdom and select countries in the Gulf Co-Op Council (GCC), namely Saudi Arabia, United Arab Emirates, and Qatar. Altogether, 29,338 employees were surveyed in 2010.

The Kenexa High Performance Institute (KHPI) operates in order to provide thought leadership for Kenexa and the HR management field and to publish research findings to disseminate intellectual capital. WorkTrends data allow Kenexa and Kenexa clients to understand findings in a more robust way.

# History

The WorkTrends survey was initiated in 1945 to supply the survey research unit of Control Data Business Advisors—the predecessor to Gantz Wiley Research—with an employee opinion normative database from which to serve its clients. In 2006, Kenexa acquired Gantz Wiley Research due to its expertise in organizational surveys and data-based action planning. Since its inception, the WorkTrends survey has been administered, via paper and pencil, nearly every year to a U.S. population of five to ten thousand employees. The survey process migrated to an online-based administration method in 2007.

# Online Sampling Procedures

Kenexa's online survey vendor for WorkTrends uses a panel sampling methodology to cultivate a large group of people in various regions of the world who are willing to take online surveys on a wide variety of topics. After seeing advertising for volunteers through website banner advertisements and links, potential panelists "opt-in," which allows our vendor to authenticate the individual's identity, name, and address through the respective country's postal service. In addition, WorkTrends data is subjected to quality protocols to ensure the data are of the highest integrity. When panelists opt-in, they answer demographic questions, which allows KHPI to select certain individuals for specific studies. Once the panel is determined, WorkTrends surveys are sent to randomly selected panel members. The sample of employees resulting from this method is demographically representative of the employees in each country who work at larger organizations. WorkTrends data allow for less sampling error and better external validity.

**WorkTrends Countries**

**Asia Pacific:** Australia, China, India, Japan

**Americas:** Brazil, Canada, Mexico, United States

**EMEA:** Denmark, Finland, France, Germany, Italy, The Netherlands, Russia, Saudi Arabia, Spain, Sweden, Switzerland, United Arab Emirates, United Kingdom

## WorkTrends Around the Globe in 2010

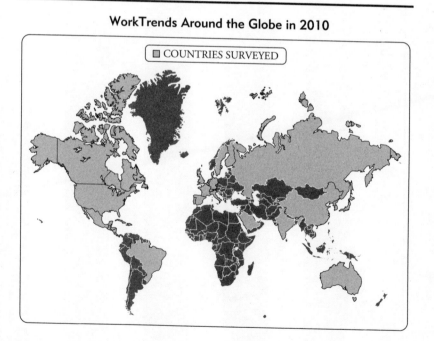

# WorkTrends 2010 Demographics

## Age

| 18–24 | 25–34 | 35–44 | 45–54 | 55+ |

## Organization Size by Number of Employees

| 100–249 | 250–499 | 500–999 | 1,000–4,999 | 5,000–9,999 | 10,000+ |

## Employee Tenure

| < 1 Year | 1–2 Years | 3–5 Years | 6–10 Years | 11–15 Years | 15+ Years |

## Job Type

| Professional/Technical | Clerical | Service/Production | Senior/Middle Management | Supervisors | Sales |

## Industry

| Government | Heavy/Light Manufacturing | Retail | Health Care Services | Banking and Financial Services | High-Tech Manufacturing |

# C

# Discovering the RESPECT Taxonomy: The Method

**W**HEN WE SET OUT to understand what workers want from their organizations, we looked to our WorkTrends data: twenty-five years of employee answers to the question, *"As an employee, what is the most important thing you want from the organization for which you work?"* Our goal was to boil down a staggering number of open-ended answers from the data set to a more manageable framework.

Much of qualitative research relies on a subjective coding process, which can result in a taxonomy reflective of a few coders' subjective paradigms and perspectives. We wanted to use a more rigorous method. We minimized the impact of any one person's perspectives by employing twenty people, "sorters," to sort our data into categories. To statistically validate the sorting process, we used the guidelines set forth in the critical incidents technique, which involves a two-phase process: an initial sort, which is an inductive process, and a re-translation sort, which is a deductive process. Through these processes, we have twenty-three independent perspectives (twenty sorters and three researchers) embedded in the taxonomy. We account for agreement and disagreement among these perspectives and check the categories three times.

## The Sample and the Sorters

From over 124,000 answers, a random sub-sample of eighteen hundred answers stratified by year and country was selected for each sorting task. This sample was drawn to provide the sorters with a manageable number of responses that were representative of employee opinions over time and from around the world. In the United States, one hundred answers were randomly sampled from multiple years: 1988, 1993, 1997, 2002, and 2008. Because international data were collected in 2008, one hundred answers were also randomly sampled from multiple countries: the United States, Canada, Mexico, Brazil, the UK, Germany, The Netherlands, Italy, Russia, India, China, Japan, Australia, and the Gulf Cooperation Council (Saudi Arabia, United Arab Emirates, Oman, Bahrain, Qatar, and Kuwait). After the random sample was selected, the data were cleaned by removing irrelevant and distracting information (that is, "I don't know" or responses that did not answer the question) and splitting multiple answers. Twenty sorters, of whom ten were assigned to the initial sorting task and ten to the retranslation sort, were recruited from within Kenexa, the Minnesota Center for Survey Research (MCSR), and the University of Minnesota, and they were paid $150 upon completion of the sort.

## Devising the Taxonomy: The Initial Sort

The initial sort is an inductive process through which sorters derive categories from the answers given. Initial sorters did a cursory read-through of the sample of answers to create preliminary categories and then re-read each answer carefully, one-by-one, and assigned each to a category. As they sorted, sorters were instructed to tweak the categories to more closely match the nature of the data. This inductive method of sorting produced evolved and finely honed categories, as well as allowed for new categories to be added to the initial list.

We collected the sorting tasks from the sorters and combined their results. We used a quantitative method, principal component analysis (PCA), to check to what extent sorters agreed on the number and nature of categories. Our goal for this step was to find the taxonomy in which raters agreed with the number and nature of the categories.

Sorted items were transformed into item-agreement matrices, and PCA was used to extract component categories. Parallel analysis suggested about twelve components, but a range of component models (from five to twelve) was extracted to explore the data.

A category definition meeting was held with several researchers to create an "Employee Want Category Codebook," wherein each category was assigned a number, title, and comprehensive definition, including what should and should not be included in the category. To achieve this, multiple PCA models were considered for factor loadings and inter-pretability. At the end of the meeting, a nine-component model had emerged, which consisted of the categories Recognition, Appreciation, and Respect; Fairness and Equality; Pay and Benefits; Growth, Development, Training, Education, Promotion, and Advancement; Positive Working Conditions (Social and Physical); Interesting and Fulfilling Work; Job Security/Stability; Communication, Feedback, Honesty, Integrity, Ethics, and Trust; and Leadership/Management (see Table C.1 for the evolution of the RESPECT taxonomy). Eventually, the edited taxonomy was finalized, integrating comments and changes made by the researchers. This finalized taxonomy was used in the retranslation sort.

# Checking the Taxonomy: The Retranslation Sort

The retranslation sort is a deductive process through which sorters assign a sub-sample of answers to predefined categories. The sub-sample for the retranslation sort was comprised of different answers and selected in the same manner as in the initial sort. Results of the retranslation

## Table C.1. The Genesis and Evolution of RESPECT

| Initial Sort Category | Retranslation Sort Category | Consensus Meeting Final Category |
|---|---|---|
| Recognition, Appreciation, Respect | Recognition, Appreciation, Respect | **Recognition** |
| Interesting and Fulfilling Work | Interesting and Fulfilling Work | **Exciting Work** |
| Job Security/Stability | Job Security/Stability | **Security of Employment** |
| Pay and Benefits | Pay and Benefits | **Pay** |
| Growth, Development, Training, Education, Promotion, Advancement | Growth, Development, Training, Education, Promotion, Advancement | **Education and Career Growth** |
| Positive Working Conditions [Social and Physical] | Positive Working Conditions [Social and Physical] | **Conditions** |
| Communication, Feedback, Honesty, Integrity, Ethics, and Trust | Communication, Feedback, Honesty, Integrity, Ethics, and Trust | **Truth** (*dropped integrity, ethics, and trust due to under 5 percent of responses, but referenced for the chapter discussion*) |
| Fairness and Equality | Fairness and Equality | *Dropped—under 5 percent of responses; category mapped to Truth and Communication* |
| Leadership/ Management | Good Leadership | *Dropped—under 5 percent of responses; generic answers were given (e.g., "good leaders") that were covered by other RESPECT elements* |
|  | Success | *Dropped—under 5 percent of responses* |

sort indicated that agreement across sorters was good and supported the taxonomy derived in the initial sort. Nearly 87 percent of items were categorized, with at least moderate agreement across sorters. Only about 4 percent of items exhibited split agreement; 9 percent exhibited poor or no agreement across sorters. These items were examined carefully in a consensus meeting.

## Finalizing the Taxonomy: The Consensus Meeting

The purpose of the consensus meeting was to discuss answers exhibiting split agreement or low agreement and to reach consensus about which category they belonged to. Problem answers were brought up one at a time and discussed. Of those items discussed, all but 2.8 percent (bad items = 2.4; foreign language translation issues = .4) were resolved by consensus. In addition, there emerged a very small, but meaningful category the researchers came to call Success. Also, during the consensus meeting, various minor changes were made to the taxonomy to help clarify the meaning of the categories and eliminate any future confusion.

In subsequent administrations of WorkTrends, a categorical list based on the qualitatively derived categories was added to the survey. Due to the small number of answers in some subcategories (under 5 percent of responses) and seeking to include major categories under which these smaller subcategories would correlate, we chose to exclude Loyalty, Trust, Integrity, and Ethics; Success; Good Leadership; and Fairness and Equality. Final category names were slightly altered to build the acronym RESPECT.

# NOTES

## Chapter 1

1. T. E. Deal and A. A. Kennedy. *Corporate Cultures* (Reading, MA: Addison-Wesley, 1982).
2. International Monetary Fund. "World Economic Outlook Database" (2010).
3. F. Herzberg, B. Mausener, R. O. Peterson, and D. F. Capwell. *Job Attitudes: Review of Research and Opinion* (Pittsburgh, PA: Psychological Services of Pittsburg, 1957).

## Chapter 2

1. J. W. Wiley, B. J. Kowske, and A. E. Herman. "Developing and validating a global model of employee engagement." In S. L. Albrecht (Ed.), *Handbook of Employee Engagement* (Northampton, MA: Edward Elgar Publishing Limited, 2010).
2. J. K. Harter, F. L. Schmidt, and T. L. Hayes. "Business-unit-level relationship between employee satisfaction, employee engagement, and business outcomes: A meta-analysis," *Journal of Applied Psychology*, 87 (2002): 268–279.

3. R. J. Vance. *Employee Engagement and Commitment: A Guide to Understanding, Measuring and Increasing Engagement in Your Organization* (Alexandria, VA: SHRM Foundation, 2006).
4. D. Robinson. "Engagement is marriage of various factors at work," *Employee Benefits* (2007): 37.
5. B. Schneider, W. H. Macey, K. M. Barbera, and N. Martin. "Driving customer satisfaction and financial success through employee engagement," *People & Strategy, 32* (2009): 22–27.
6. J. W. Wiley, B. J. Kowske, and A. E. Herman. "Developing and validating a global model of employee engagement." In S. L. Albrecht (Ed.), *Handbook of Employee Engagement* (Northampton, MA: Edward Elgar Publishing Limited, 2010).
7. EEI $\alpha = 0.91$
8. B. Schneider and D. E. Bowen. "Employee and customer perceptions of service in banks: Replication and extension," *Journal of Applied Psychology, 70* (1985): 423–433.
9. POI $\alpha = 0.77$
10. The RESPECT Index is computed by (1) averaging the percent favorable scores for each RESPECT category, if the category has more than one item, and then (2) averaging the category scores across all seven RESPECT categories, resulting in one final RESPECT Index score. As before, percent favorable is computed as the percent of respondents who agree or strongly agree with the item. Statistical analyses on the resulting RESPECT Index revealed a high level of internal consistency reliability ($\alpha = .0.91$).
11. American Customer Service Index. "Economic Indicator." (n.d.) Retrieved at www.theacsi.org/index.php?option=com_content&view=article&id=47&Itemid=123 February 25, 2011.

## Chapter 3

1. R. Eisenherger, P. Fasolo, and V. Davis-LaMastro. "Perceived organizational support and employee diligence, commitment, and innovation," *Journal of Applied Psychology, 75* (1990): 51–59.
2. F. Luthans and A. Stajkovic. "Reinforce for performance: The need to go beyond pay and even rewards," *Academy of Management Executive, 13* (1999): 49–57.
3. A. Stajkovic and F. Luthans. "A meta-analysis of the effects of organizational behavior modification on task performance 1975–1995," *Academy of Management Journal, 40* (1997): 1122–1149.
4. It's important to recognize at the outset that all employees, from all industries, and in all types of positions, desire each element of the RESPECT list.

The archetypes we use in this book, like Ann, represent the type of employee who mentions a particular element more than his or her working peers do.

5. "Generation Next changes the face of the workplace," *The NewsHour with Jim Lehrer* (2006).

6. B. Kaye and S. Jordan-Evans. *Love 'Em or Lose 'Em: Getting Good People to Stay* (San Francisco: Berrett-Koehler, 2005).

7. T. Schwartz. "The productivity paradox. How Sony Pictures gets more out of people by demanding less," *Harvard Business Review*, 88 (2010): 65–69.

8. K. Luthans. "Recognition: A powerful, but often overlooked, leadership tool to improve employee performance," *Journal of Leadership & Organizational Studies*, 7 (2000): 31–39.

9. L. Shepherd. "Special report on rewards and recognition: Getting personal," *Workforce Management* (2010), www.workforce.com/section/benefits-compensation/features/special-report-rewards-recognition-getting-personal/index.html.

10. V. Uyen. "Managers don't dole out recognition as often as they should: Survey," *Canadian HR Reporter*, 19 (2006): 23, 25–26.

11. K. Luthans. "Recognition: A powerful, but often overlooked, leadership tool to improve employee performance," *Journal of Leadership & Organizational Studies*, 7 (2000): 31–39.

12. L. Shepherd. "On recognition, multinationals think globally," *Workforce Management* (2010), www.workforce.com/section/benefits-compensation/archive/feature-recognition-multinationals-think-globally/273823.html.

13. L. Shepherd. "Special report on rewards and recognition: Getting personal," *Workforce Management* (2010), www.workforce.com/section/benefits-compensation/features/special-report-rewards-recognition-getting-personal/index.html.

14. B. Kaye and S. Jordan-Evans. *Love 'Em or Lose 'Em: Getting Good People to Stay* (San Francisco: Berrett-Koehler, 2005).

15. B. James. "Motivation: Separate ways," *Employee Benefits* (2010): 41–43.

16. L. Shepherd. "On recognition, multinationals think globally," *Workforce Management* (2010), www.workforce.com/section/benefits-compensation/archive/feature-recognition-multinationals-think-globally/273823.html.

17. E. Frauenheim. "Staying the course: Sticking to the talent plan at Caterpillar, Coca-Cola, and McDonald's," *Workforce Management* (2009), www.workforce.com/archive/feature/hr-management/staying-course-sticking-talent-plan-at/index.php?htm.

18. L. Shepherd. "Special report on rewards and recognition: Getting personal," *Workforce Management* (2010), www.workforce.com/section/benefits-compensation/features/special-report-rewards-recognition-getting-personal/index.html.

19. E. Frauenheim. "Myriad avenues to stellar service," *Workforce Management* (2010), www.workforce.com/archive/freatures/27/30/30/index.php.

## Chapter 4

1. R. J. House and L. A. Wigdor. "Herzberg's dual-factor theory of job satisfaction and motivation: A review of the evidence and a criticism," *Personnel Psychology*, *20* (1967): 369–390.
2. J. Dewey. *Democracy and Education* (Mineola, NY: Courier Dover Publications, 2004).
3. B. Kaye and S. Jordan-Evans. "Engaging the massive middle." [White paper] (2007), www.careersystemsintl.com/White_Papers.asp.
4. P. Bronson. *What Should I Do with My Life?* (New York: Random House, 2002).
5. K. K. Spors. "Top small workplaces 2009," *The Wall Street Journal* (2009).
6. D. Champion. "Mastering the value chain: An interview with Mark Levin of Millennium Pharmaceuticals," *Harvard Business Review*, *79* (2001): 109–115.
7. K. K. Spors. "Top small workplaces 2009," *The Wall Street Journal* (2009).
8. E. Frauenheim, "Making the call for themselves," *Workforce Management* (2010), www.workforce.com/archive/feature/training-development/making-call-themselves/index.php?htm.
9. B. Schneider, W. H. Macey, K. M. Barbera, and N. Martin. "Driving customer satisfaction and financial success through employee engagement," *People & Strategy*, *32* (2009): 22–27.
10. Ibid.
11. J. C. Spender and B. Strong, "Who has innovative ideas? Employees," *The Wall Street Journal* (2010), http://online.wsj.com/article/SB100014240527 487041006045751460833310500518.html?mod&mg=com-wsj.
12. E. Frauenheim. "Can Zappo's corporate culture survive the Amazon jungle?" *Workforce Management* (2009), www.workforce.com/archive/feature/hr-management/can-zappos-corporate-culture-survive-amazon-jungle/index.php?ht=

## Chapter 5

1. A. H. Maslow. "A theory of human motivation," *Psychological Review*, *50* (1943): 370–396.
2. M. Sverke, J. Hellgren, and K. Naswall. "No security: A meta-analysis and review of job insecurity and its consequences," *Journal of Occupational Health Psychology*, *7* (2002): 242–64.

3. G. L. Cheng and D. K. S. Chan. "Who suffers more from job insecurity: A meta-analytic review," *Applied Psychology: An International Review*, *57*(2008): 272–303.

4. U. Kinnunen, T. Feldt, and A. Mauno. "Job insecurity and self-esteem: Evidence from cross-lagged relations in a one-year longitudinal sample," *Personality and Individual Differences*, *35* (2003): 617–632.

5. S. J. Ashford, C. Lee, and P. Bobko. "Content, causes, and consequences of job insecurity: A theory based measure and substantive test," *Academy of Management Journal*, *32* (1989): 803–829.

6. U. Kinnunen, T. Feldt, and A. Mauno. "Job insecurity and self-esteem: Evidence from cross-lagged relations in a one-year longitudinal sample," *Personality and Individual Differences*, *35* (2003): 617–632.

7. R. C. Mayer, J. H. Davis, and F. D. Schoorman. "An integrative model of organizational trust," *Academy of Management Review*, *20* (1995): 709–734.

8. Fair or adequate pay is not mentioned in the drivers of job security; rather, we see that employees want to know that their contributions are valued. This means that job security is less about income and more about a belief that decision-makers can recognize an employee's contribution (especially when layoffs are looming).

9. C. Leonard and C. S. Rugaber. "Government job security vanishes," *Deseret News* (2010), www.deseretnews.com/article/700045443/Government-job-security-vanishes.html.

10. J. S. Lublin. "Message to CEOs: Do more to keep your key employees," *The Wall Street Journal* (2010), http://online.wsj.com/article/SB1000142405274 8703886904576031902249606570.html?KEYWORDS=Message+to+CEOs%3A+Do+More+to+Keep+Your+Key+Employees.

11. M. Whitehouse. "Some firms struggle to hire despite high unemployment," *The Wall Street Journal* (2010), http://online.wsj.com/article/SB10001424052748704895004575395491314812452.html?mod=WSJ_article_related.

12. E. Zhao. "Faces—and fates—of the jobless," *The Wall Street Journal* (2010), http://online.wsj.com/article/SB10001424052748704271804575405463495941570.html?KEYWORDS=job+security+layoff.

13. C. Dougherty. "Faces—and fates—of the jobless," *The Wall Street Journal* (2010), http://online.wsj.com/article/SB10001424052748704271804575405463495941570.html?KEYWORDS=job+security+layoff.

14. J. Light. "Faces—and fates—of the jobless," *The Wall Street Journal* (2010), http://online.wsj.com/article/SB10001424052748704271804575405463495941570.html?KEYWORDS=job+security+layoff.

15. S. Murray. "Faces—and fates—of the jobless," *The Wall Street Journal* (2010), http://online.wsj.com/article/SB10001424052748704271804575 405463495941570.html?KEYWORDS=job+security+layoff.

16. W. F. Cascio. *"Strategies for responsible restructuring,"* Academy of Management Executive, *16* (2002): 80–91.

17. _____, "Employment downsizing: Causes, costs, and consequences." In L. Stadtler, A. Schmitt, P. Klarner, and T. Straub (Eds.), *More Than Bricks in the Wall: Organizational Perspectives for Sustainable Success* (Wiesbaden, Germany: Gabler, 2010).

18. F. Koller. *Spark: How Old-Fashioned Values Drive a Twenty-First Century Corporation* (New York: Public Affairs, 2010).

19. K. K. Spors. "Top small workplaces 2009," *The Wall Street Journal* (2009), http://online.wsj.com/article/SB10001424052970204731804574384600167797142.html.

20. R. G. Matthews. "Jobs begin to sprout: One Arkansas town underlines U.S. employment trend," *The Wall Street Journal* (2010), http://online.wsj.com/article/SB10001424052702304830104575172062762799460.html.

21. V. Salemi. "Job stability is the new black," *Forbes*, www.forbes.com/2009/10/21/job-security-flexibility-forbes-woman-net-worth-personal-brand.html.

## Chapter 6

1. A. H. Maslow. "A theory of human motivation," *Psychological Review, 50* (1943): 370–396.

2. S. Miller. "Most U.S. employers expect to give pay raises in 2011." Alexandria, VA: Society for Human Resource Management (2010), www.shrm.org/hrdisciplines/compensation/Articles/Pages/2011Raises.aspx

3. Ibid.

4. M. L. Williams, H. H. Brown, L. R. Ford, L. J. Williams, and S. M. Carraher. "A comprehensive model and measure of compensation satisfaction," *Journal of Occupational and Organizational Psychology, 81* (2010): 639–668.

5. F. Herzberg, B. Mausener, R. O. Peterson, and D. F. Capwell. *Job Attitudes: Review of Research and Opinion* (Pittsburgh, PA: Psychological Services of Pittsburg, 1957).

6. D. G. Jenkins, A. Mitra, N. Gupta, and J. D. Shaw. "Are financial incentives related to performance? A meta-analytic review of empirical research," *Journal of Applied Psychology, 83* (1998): 777–787.

7. J. Igalens and P. Roussel. "A study of the relationship between compensation package, work motivation, and job satisfaction," *Journal of Organizational Behavior, 20* (1999): 1003–1025.

8. R. L. Schuler and N. Rogovsky. "Understanding compensation practice variations across firms: The impact of national culture," *Journal of International Business Studies, 29* (1998): 159–177.

9. "Annual wages were calculated by multiplying monthly wages by 12, weekly wages by 52, daily wages by 5 x 52 and hourly wages by W x 52, where W is the legal maximum (or the practical, if lower) workweek length in hours. A purchasing power parity (PPP) conversion rate from 2009—obtained from the International Monetary Fund (IMF)'s World Economic Outlook Database, October 2010 Edition—was used to convert the annual wage from national currency to international dollars." Where there was a range of minimum wages, the lowest was used in the annual wage calculation. Those with asterisks are not federally mandated, but rather represent commonly negotiated wages between a combination of labor and unions, employers, and/or government.

10. "List of minimum wages by country," Wikipedia (2010), http://en.wikipedia.org/wiki/List_of_minimum_wages_by_country.

11. L. Christie. "Poverty in the U.S. spikes," *CNNMoney* (2010), http://money.cnn.com/2010/09/16/news/economy/Census_poverty_rate/index.htm.

12. "Consumer Expenditure Survey 2006– 2007 (Report 1021)." (Washington, DC: U.S. Bureau of Labor Statistics, 2010).

13. B. J. Kowske. "Does money motivate?" *Evolve, 2.2* (2008): 22–24.

14. J. Krasner. "Blue Cross CEO's pay rose 26%," *The Boston Globe* (2009), www.boston.com/business/healthcare/articles/2009/02/28/blue_cross_ceos_pay_rose_26/

15. B. Sopelsa. "Biggest executive bonuses of the past decade," CNBC (2009), www.cnbc.com/id/33534042/Biggest_Executive_Bonuses_of_the_Past_Decade.

16. *The World Factbook.* (Washington, DC: CIA, 2010).

17. Correlation for the international sample of executives between rating of organizational improvement in the past twelve months and rating of pay: r = .41; p < .001

18. D. J. Wudyka. "What is "fair" pay?" (London: Westminster Associates, 2006), www.westminsterassociates.com/media_news_fairplay.htm.

19. "The business case for fair pay," Fair Pay Network, www.fairpaynetwork.org/?page=case_for_business.

20. S. Needleman. "Should a business offer paid maternity leave?" *The Wall Street Journal* (2010), http://online.wsj.com/article/SB10001424052748704293604575343332721123208.html?KEYWORDS=fair+compensation.

21. Ibid.

22. World Business Council for Sustainable Development. "Novartis: Implementing a living wage globally" (2007), www.wbcsd.org/DocRoot/

wL5MwRTJXZ0aZW6NaFon/novartis_implementing_a_living_wage_
full_case_web.pdf.

23. K. K. Spors. "Top small workplaces 2009," *The Wall Street Journal* (2009).


# Chapter 7

1. U.S. Department of Education. *Digest of Education* (NCES 2010–2013, 2009).
2. A. Adler. "Individual psychology," *The Journal of Abnormal and Social Psychology, 22* (1927): 116–122.
3. A. Adler. *Superiority and Social Interest* (New York: Norton, 1979).
4. A. H. Maslow. "A theory of human motivation," *Psychological Review, 50* (1943): 370–396.
5. S. L. Rynes, B. Gerhart, and P. Laura. "Personnel psychology: Performance evaluation and pay for performance," *Annual Review of Psychology, 56* (2005): 571–600.
6. A. Tziner and A. Birati. "Assessing employee turnover costs," *Human Resource Management Review, 6* (1996): 113–122.
7. M. A. Royal. "Strategies for retaining top talent," *Human Resource Executive Online* (2009), www.hreonline.com/hre/story.jsp?storyid=250194739.
8. Employment Policy Foundation. "A brief look at contemporary issues in employment and workplace policy" (Washington, DC, 2004).
9. J. W. Wiley. *Strategic Employee Surveys* (San Francisco: Jossey-Bass, 2010).
10. L. J. Bassi, L. Jens, D. P. McMurrer, and M. Van Buren. "Profiting from learning: Firm-level effects of training investments and market implications," *Singapore Management Review, 24* (2002): 61–76.
11. Although years of birth slightly vary based on source, for this effort we used delineations put forth by Strauss and Howe (1991) in their book *Generations: The History of America's Future, 1584 to 2069.* Baby Boomers were born in the years 1943–1960, Generation X in 1961–1981, and Millennials in 1982–1991.
12. U.S. Census Bureau, in 2006– 2008 American Community Survey, Population Estimates (2008).
13. R. Silverman http://blogs.wsj.com/juggle/2010/09/28/slow-progress-for-women-in-management/
14. The White House Project. *The White House Project Report: Benchmarking Women's Leadership* (New York: The White House Project, 2009).
15. L. Sullivan and J. Zaino. "People first: Talent development is a Wal-Mart hallmark," *Information Week* (2004), www.informationweek.com/news/global-cio/outsourcing/showArticle.jhtml?articleID=47902700.

16. *Workforce Management* Editors. "2009 Optimas Awards," *Workforce Management* (2009), www.workforce.com/archive/feature/optimas-awards/2009-optimas-award-winners/index.php.

17. G. Ruiz. "Kimberly-Clark developing talent in developing markets," *Workforce Management* (2006), www.workforce.com/archive/feature/kimberly-clark-developing-talent-developing-world-markets/243354.php.

18. *Workforce Management* Editors. "2009 Optimas Awards," *Workforce Management* (2009), www.workforce.com/archive/feature/optimas-awards/2009-optimas-award-winners/index.php.

19. P. J. Kieger. "Gensler: Optimas Award winner for managing change," *Workforce Management* (2009), www.workforce.com/archive/feature/training-development/gensler-optimas-award-winner-managing-change/index.php.

20. C. Huff. "Special report on training and development: Powering up a Hispanic workforce," *Workforce Management* (2009), www.workforce.com/archive/feature/training-development/special-report-training-development-powering-up-a/index.php.

## Chapter 8

1. Note that WorkTrends is an online survey, which means that respondents have access to a computer. This sample may not adequately represent the working poor, who are more likely to work in unsafe or poor conditions.

2. The WorkTrends survey from which trend data were derived was revised over the years, with survey items removed and added. All trend data available for the country or countries specified are presented for each trend line discussed in this book.

3. Please note the longer gap between 1997 and 2005. All data collected is reported.

4. D. Jolly. "Taking the boss hostage? In France, it's a labor tactic," *The New York Times* (2009), http://nytimes.com/2009/04/03/business/global/03labor.html.

5. *The World Factbook: China* (Washington, DC: CIA, est. 2008) vs. WorkTrends (2010) in industry segments: Agriculture: 39.5 percent vs. .8 percent; Production or "Industry" 27.2 percent vs. 35 percent; Service 33.2 percent vs. 20 percent. From World Bank 2009 vs. WorkTrends 2010—percent of women in labor force: 45 percent vs. 49.6 percent. *The World Factbook: India* (Washington, DC: CIA, est. 2009) vs. WorkTrends (2010): Agriculture 52 percent vs. .2 percent; Production or "Industry" 14 percent vs. 26 percent; Service 34 percent vs. 32 percent. From World Bank 2009 vs. WorkTrends 2010— percent of women in labor force: 28 percent vs. 39.8 percent.

6. *The World Factbook: India.* (Washington, DC: CIA, 2007). www.cia. gov/library/publications/the-world-factbook/index.html.

7. *The World Factbook: China.* (Washington, DC: CIA, 2007). www.cia.gov/library/publications/the-world-factbook/index.html.

8. The World Bank (2009). "Labor force, female (% of total labor force)". Data retrieved at http://data.worldbank.org/indicator/SL.TLF.TOTL.FE.ZS on May 18, 2011.

9. E. Beck. "Offices that work. Four entrepreneurs create spaces with impact," *BusinessWeek* (2007), www.businessweek.com/magazine/content/07_26/b4040401.htm.

10. Pearson correlation, one-tailed r = 0.417, p < .001

11. Pearson correlation, one-tailed r = 0.497, p < .001

## Chapter 9

1. R. C. Mayer, J. H. Davis, and F. D. Schoorman. "An integrative model of organizational trust," *Academy of Management Review, 20* (1995): 709–734.

2. D. M. Rousseau, S. B. Sitkin, R.S. Burt, and C. Camerer. "Not so different after all: A cross-discipline view of trust," *Academy of Management Review 23* (1998): 393–404.

3. S. M. Norman, B. J. Avolio, and F. Luthans. "The impact of positivity and transparency on trust in leaders and their perceived effectiveness," *The Leadership Quarterly, 21* (2010): 350–364.

4. L. Reave. "Spiritual values and practices related to leadership effectiveness," *The Leadership Quarterly, 16* (2005): 655–687.

5. J. O'Toole and W. Bennis. "What's needed next: A culture of candor," *Harvard Business Review, 87* (2009): 54–61.

6. V. Viswesvaran and F. L. Schmidt. "Comprehensive meta-analysis of integrity test validities: Findings and implications for personnel selection and theories of job performance," *Journal of Applied Psychology, 78* (1993): 679–703.

7. A. Verghese, to 2010, http://blogs.wsj.com/indiarealtime/2010/09/14/chief-mentor-building-leadership-credibility/.

8. T. Schwarz. "The productivity paradox. How Sony Pictures gets more out of people by demanding less," *Harvard Business Review, 88* (2010): 65–69.

9. J. McGregor. "The employee is always right," *BusinessWeek* (2007), www.businessweek.com/magazine/content/07_47/b4059064.htm?chan= search.

10. A. Lyman. "SAS Institute: #1 company to work for in America" [White Paper], (2010), http://resources.greatplacetowork.com/article/pdf/sas_2010 .pdf.

11. K. K. Spors. "Top small workplaces 2009," *The Wall Street Journal* (2009).
12. F. Koller. *Spark: How Old-Fashioned Values Drive a Twenty-First Century Corporation* (New York: Public Affairs, 2010).
13. G. Kranz. "A nonprofit's investments in leadership development pay off," *Workforce Management* (2010), www.workforce.com/archive/feature/26/96/21/index.php?ht=

## Chapter 10

1. It's important to realize that when we say "bureaucracy" we aren't just talking about government entities. Bureaucracies exist in the private and non-profit sector, while some government agencies have proven to be very dynamic.
2. J. S. Lublin. "Message to CEOs: Do more to keep your key employees," *The Wall Street Journal* (2010), http://online.wsj.com/article/SB1000142405274 87038869045760319022249606570.html?KEYWORDS=Message+to+CEOs%3A+Do+More+to+Keep+Your+Key+Employees.
3. Bersin & Associates. "New Bersin & Associates research shows global growth creating a new war for talent" (2011), www.bersin.com/News/Content.aspx?id=13723.

# ABOUT THE AUTHORS

Jack Wiley, Ph.D., is founder and executive director of the Kenexa High Performance Institute. He has been researching and surveying employee opinions for more than thirty-five years and is internationally recognized for his groundbreaking research, which links employee opinions to customer satisfaction and business performance. He is also the creator of the WorkTrends™ survey, an exhaustive international research program that produces results featured in both scholarly studies and the popular press worldwide. A firm believer in developing employee talent to the fullest extent, Dr. Wiley has used the knowledge absorbed from his lifetime of research to help create meaningful organization development programs for the health care, financial services, manufacturing, and retail industries.

Wiley was elected as a Fellow in the Society for Industrial and Organizational Psychology, the American Psychological Association, and the Association for Psychological Science. He holds a doctorate in organizational psychology from the University of Tennessee, is a licensed consulting psychologist, and has received accreditation as a senior professional in human resources (SPHR). Dr. Wiley was the founder and CEO of Gantz Wiley Research, a survey research consulting firm specializing in employee and customer surveys for corporate clients, acquired by Kenexa in 2006. He is also the author of *Strategic Employee Surveys: Using Evidence-Based Guidelines for Driving Organizational Success*, published in 2010.

**Brenda Kowske, Ph.D.,** is a research manager and consultant for the Kenexa High Performance Institute and the manager of the Institute's WorkTrends™ study, the annual survey of over thirty-five thousand employees worldwide. She specializes in conducting valid and reliable research that informs talent decisions to improve organizational performance. What are the driving forces behind a stellar leadership team around the world? What motivates employees to engage in and excel at their work? Dr. Kowske has the answers.

Throughout her career in leadership and research consulting, she has tailored online survey processes for strategic decision making and workforce insight. She has created valid performance measurement systems that differentiate employees and has conducted talent analytics for compensation, promotion, and development decisions. Dr. Kowske has published numerous book chapters, white papers, and articles for academic and professional journals, most recently "Millennials' (lack of) attitude problem: An empirical examination of generational effects on work attitudes" in the *Journal of Business and Psychology*. She is a member of the Academy of Management, Academy of Human Resource Development, American Psychological Association, and the Society for Industrial and Organizational Psychology. Dr. Kowske holds a doctorate in human resource development and a master of education from the University of Minnesota. Each year, Dr. Kowske acts as lead author of the Institute's Annual Report, most recently the 2010 volume, *Exploring Leadership and Managerial Effectiveness*.

# INDEX